"Fill 'er Up"

An Architectural History of America's Gas Stations

by Daniel I. Vieyra

with a Foreword by James Marston Fitch

"Fill 'er Up"

Collier Books
A Division of Macmillan Publishing Co., Inc.
NEW YORK
Collier Macmillan Publishers
LONDON

Macmillan Publishing Co., Inc.
866 Third Avenue, New York, N.Y. 10022
Collier Macmillan Canada, Ltd.

Library of Congress Cataloging in Publication Data
Vieyra, Daniel I.
    "Fill 'er Up".
    Includes index.
    1.   Automobiles—Service stations—United States—
History.   2.   Architecture, Commercial—United States—
History.   I.   Title.
TL153.V53   725'.38   79-19418
ISBN 0-02-622000-8
ISBN 0-02-007400-X pbk.

First Collier Books Edition 1979

"Fill 'er Up" is also published in a hardcover edition by
Macmillan Publishing Co., Inc.

Printed in the United States of America

To Katherine who lives with gas stations,
and Siegfried who lives for them.

Contents

Foreword

No technological development in modern American history has had so pervasive an effect upon our culture as the internal combustion engine. The rise of the automobile all but drove out of existence one of the world's greatest railroad systems (just as that system had earlier eliminated the great nineteenth-century system of canal and river transportation). The automobile has had a profound, and generally disastrous, impact upon older American cities, creating in their stead a new type of urban settlement exemplified by Los Angeles, Houston, the Las Vegas "strip," and upper-class exurbia. Not surprisingly the auto quickly began generating a new range of building types, including the motel, the fast-food franchise eatery, the drive-in bank, the suburban shopping mall, and the multistory parking garage. Even today, when the soaring cost of gasoline seems certain to restrict and eventually reduce the car's future influence, the private auto remains the absolutely dominant form of American transportation.

This auto-centered growth has, of course, not gone unrecognized or unrecorded. Indeed, it has generated an enormous literature of both attack and defense. But, oddly enough, little if any of this literature has been authentically historiographic. Instead, the sheer presence of the auto has been handled as if it were an ongoing natural force, like gravity or tidal action. The tacit acceptance of the automobile and the changes it has caused the built environment to undergo are doubly strange when we stop to realize that many of the forms which it generated are now old enough to justify consideration as historic artifacts. It is, after all, only seventy years since the first factory-made automobiles appeared on American roads (and many of these older machines have already achieved the prestige and value of "genuine antiques").

If architectural historians have not yet found auto-generated structures worthy of more than peripheral study, their impact has not gone unobserved by other chroniclers of our culture. Sinclair Lewis suggested that work in a filling station was the best vantage point from which to study American culture.

Appropriately, the gas station has come to play a symbolic role in the arts. John Steinbeck's writings (*The Grapes of Wrath*), Elizabeth Bishop's poetry ("Filling Station"), and Lew Christensen's ballet choreography (*Filling Station*) have all used the building as a representation of Americana. Artists such as Edward Hopper painted the gas station as an integral part of the landscape, while more recently Edward Ruscha, John Baeder, and Allan D'Arcangelo have singled it out as an element worthy of more detailed study.

It is obvious that Daniel Vieyra has become very fond of the subject of his investigation. But his lighthearted text should not conceal the serious research which has gone into it. The reader need not share completely his enthusiasm for the vernacular aesthetics of the gas station in order to agree with him that it constitutes an organic part of the material culture of our times. As such, the gas station is entitled to the same curatorial attention that is normally reserved for older, more urbane and more elite artifacts.

One of the most fascinating aspects of modern cultural history is its continually accelerating rate of change; unfortunately, one of the greatest hazards for contemporary historians and preservationists is their tendency to forget this crucial fact when deciding what to record, what to preserve, and what to throw away. For, if the past is any index to such matters, the time is not far away when a 1920s filling station, complete with hand-operated pumps and 19¢-a-gallon fuel, will be as rare an artifact as the 1840 general stores and apothecaries which are now cherished exhibits in our outdoor architectural museums.

Thus, when Daniel Vieyra writes this history of the rise of the American gas station, he is perhaps even more prescient than he realizes: A new interest in the gas station's past is perhaps a subtle indication of its questionable future. Young scholars of Vieyra's generation are the first to see the buildings which the automobile has generated as a fit subject for scholarly research. His own training in historic preservation permits him to see the gas station not only as a distinct building type with its own phylogenetic development but also as an addition to the growing ranks of our endangered species.

James Marston Fitch

Graduate Program in Historic Preservation
Columbia University
April 1979

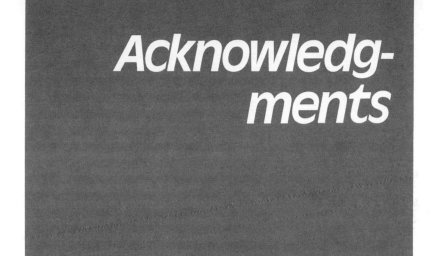

Acknowledg-
ments

This book would not have been possible without Peter C. Papademetriou who opened my eyes to gas stations.

This book began as a design studio project at the Columbia University School of Architecture's historic preservation program. I am deeply indebted to Professor James Marston Fitch for his continuing support. Thanks are also due to: David DeLong, who encouraged me to pursue gas station adaptive reuse as a studio project; Robert A. M. Stern, for his ongoing interest; Adolf K. Placzek, for teaching me the basics of scholarly research and for being flexible enough to apply these fundamentals to gas stations; William G. Foulks and Frank E. Sanchis, for moral support.

My classmates in Columbia University's 1975–76 historic preservation program provided much help and encouragement, bringing to my attention many noteworthy gas stations across the country. Taking a special interest were Henry Ayon, Minette Bickel, Andrew Dolkart, Gregory Free, Kyle Johnson, and Dale Lauren.

I owe a special debt of gratitude to Steven Izenour, for making available the comprehensive research collected for "Signs of Life: Symbols in the American City," organized and designed by Venturi and Rauch, Architects and Planners, for presentation at the Renwick Gallery of the Smithsonian Institution.

I am grateful to David Gebhard, Paul Goldberger, and William D. Brookover for their provocative insights and analysis of the material.

Synthesizing all the material would have been impossible without my wife Katherine. Her repeated readings of the manuscript and her comments on its various versions proved invaluable.

Those who have generously given information and photographs, and who have shared the romance of gas stations include: Paul David Robinson, who sacrificed much for the project; Gary Herbert Wolf, who selflessly shared his exhaustive study "The Gasoline Station: The Evolution of a Building Type as Illustrated Through a History of the Sun Oil Company Gasoline Station"; Richard J. S. Gutman; Paul W. Ivory; Peter H. Smith; Stuart E. Cohen; Wayne Attoe; H. Roger Grant; Chester H. Liebs; Thomas S. Hines; Keith A. Sculle; Eric N. Delony; Richard Stapleford; Lucien Burstein; and Martin Greif.

Others graciously responding to queries for information and lending moral and technical support were: Thomas Jefferson Eby III; Paul Goeldner; Melvin H. Goelder; Tom Martinson; Terry L. Karshner; Carole Rifkind; Janann Strand; Barbara Reed; Elizabeth Bidwell Bates; Mrs. Chester Kass; Carol Kingsbury; Joyce Hartman; Marjorie Mathes; Richard Pankratz of the Kansas State Historical Society; the North Carolina Department of Archives and History; the Rock County Historical Society; the Kling partnership of Philadelphia.

Special thanks to Stephen Edward Moskowitz, who devoted many weekends to photographing gas stations.

The research for this book could not have been complete without the oil companies, who kept in their archives the greatest wealth of information on gas stations. Past employees of petroleum companies documented their gas stations and present employees searched through corporate archives to supply me with information and photographs. Those which

xii

have been especially helpful in the compilation of this book are: Continental Oil; Exxon, USA; Gulf Oil; Mobil Oil; Shell Oil; Standard Oil of Indiana; Sun Oil; Texaco; Union 76 (division of Union Oil). Thanks also to *National Petroleum News*, McGraw-Hill Publications, which made available back issues of the magazine and their photograph collection.

Other organizations that have generously provided material include: Avery Architectural Library at Columbia University, especially Nevelle Thompson, Charling Fagan and Carol Falcione; Fondren Library at Rice University, especially Fern B. Hyman, James R. Mullins, Richard H. Perrine and Charles M. Gibson; Historic American Building Survey and Historic American Engineering Record; the Library of Congress, especially Mary Ison and C. Ford Peatross; the National Register of Historic Places; the National Trust for Historic Preservation, especially Diane Maddex and Nancy A. Melin; the Newark, New Jersey Public Library, especially William J. Dane.

I also acknowledge Steve Weaver and Terry Kilpatrick. I have been fortunate to have as my editor Toni Lopopolo, without whose effervescence and dedication *"Fill 'er Up"* would have been an entirely different book.

Finally, I am grateful to my parents, Bernard and Rosita, and to my sister Marie Anne, for their consistent encouragement and enthusiasm even when the outlook was bleak; and Walter and Phyllis Raab, for their help, hospitality, and home-cooking during a seemingly endless succession of working weekends devoted to gas stations. Also thanks to Michael, David, Larry, and Vicki.

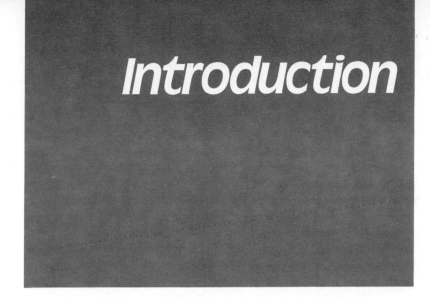

During this century, the widespread adoption of the automobile has brought radical changes to the American environment. As a result, our surroundings can no longer be referred to as landscape, but more accurately should be termed "carscape" or "motorscape." The emergence of a drive-in culture —diners, motels, roadside stands, drive-in movies and franchise food establishments—reflects the altered life-styles the automobile has created. Ironically, however, this culture, which so affects our daily lives, is taken very much for granted.

The gas station, the first structure built in response to the automobile, is undoubtedly the most widespread type of commercial building in America, and yet it is also the most ignored. Its very ubiquity allows the motorist to screen out its image. The gas station embodies architectural and cultural dimensions that most of us tend to overlook. In recent years it has been noted that "the history of architecture must not be confined to masterpieces. . . . The subject is much bigger and comprises all that man has done . . . to shape the environment." Perhaps an examination of the gas station will transform its dubious perception by the motorist into an appreciation of its imagery.

The gas station is one of the few building types that has been standardized and distributed across the entire country. It has become a sophisticated reflection of American ideals as viewed by large oil companies. At the same time, through community control and regulation of commercial buildings (controls often aimed at the gas station in particular), the service station has projected images that the communities themselves deem desirable. Echoing larger movements in architecture, gas stations are often the only examples of current design trends in areas isolated from the architectural mainstream.

The gas station, as one of the most important building types of our drive-in culture, requires its own unique method of analysis. The traditional methods of the art historian might lend themselves to the study of a Gothic cathedral or a Renaissance-inspired Stanford White townhouse. But—

whether a strictly chronological examination or a detailed stylistic analysis—such methods are not appropriate to our study of American gas stations, for they would in many ways limit our understanding of this building type. For a strictly chronological examination to be successful, there must be a clear logical development in terms of the building's function and style. There has been, however, no functional evolution of the gas station, but rather a cyclical reappearance of functional developments. Nor did station design evolve through a series of stylistic themes. A study that relied on these traits would become disjointed and encyclopedic, destroying the fun of looking at gas stations.

Analyses along the lines of those applied to traditional architectural styles would place unfair standards on this building type. The gas station was rarely an architectural trend-setter. Geared to the fast-moving traveler, its details were either crude or nonexistent; creating a single effect or image was of utmost importance. Considering the gas station in the same terms as high-style architecture would be to examine it from a distorted perspective.

One of the first to recognize the potential importance of our roadside architecture was Henry-Russell Hitchcock, who in 1936 said, "The combination of strict functionalism and bold symbolism in the best roadside stands provides, perhaps, the most encouraging sign for the architecture of the mid-twentieth century." Not until the 1960s did architects and theorists deal with the importance of the gas station and other drive-in buildings in a comprehensive manner.

Using the drive-in culture as a point of departure, architects Robert Venturi, Denise Scott Brown, and Stephen Izenour developed the concepts of "architecture as symbol" and the "architecture of communication." In contrast to the more traditional, pedestrian-oriented "architecture of space and form," such buildings are capable of conveying meaning, of making for example an instantly recognizable statement to the motorist as he speeds past. These architects and their followers contend that an examination of popular culture could make our architecture more responsive to the changing needs of people in an auto-oriented environment.

Charles Moore acknowledged the importance of roadside building in his plea for an "architecture of inclusion." David Gehbard has played a vital role in relating these current architectural theories to the histories of roadside building types.

Accepting the premise that "symbol dominates space," it becomes evident that gas stations must be examined in terms of the images or symbols that they convey to the motorist. Building on this solid theoretical foundation, this book attempts a comprehensive examination not only of the functional history of the American gasoline station but of the various images the station has projected throughout its colorful history.

"Fill 'er Up"

Beginnings 1

The modern gas station did not burst full-blown upon the American scene. Early gas stations appeared in the first decade of the twentieth century, not as sophisticated designs but as simple, ad hoc solutions to the problem of gasoline distribution. By the late teens, American automobile manufacturers had developed efficient assembly-line production methods that enabled them to sell vast numbers of Americans sturdy, inexpensive cars. It wasn't long before the automobile became a national institution. Some families mortgaged their homes in order to finance an auto. Rural families bought cars even before they installed indoor plumbing. When asked why her family owned a car but not a bathtub, one farm wife replied briskly, "Why, you can't go to town in a bathtub!"

With the popularization of the automobile, the market for automotive petroleum burgeoned. This took the oil companies by surprise. What had been a waste product of the kerosene industry suddenly became a valuable commodity. The rudimentary kerosene distribution system was hard put to accommodate the new market. From this need developed a building type that would become a ubiquitous cultural landmark: the gasoline station.

Gasoline had to pass through many stages before it reached the fuel tank of a "Tin Lizzie" or "Merry Old Olds." From the refinery where it was produced, it first went to a bulk station, usually located on the outskirts of town. The petroleum was stored in huge cylindrical tanks resting on frames high above the ground. From them, it was gravity-fed into horse-drawn tank wagons which transported the product to the local livery, general repair shop, or dry goods store. Here motorists purchased gasoline by the bucketful. They could also buy it from vendors who wandered the streets pushing small tank carts. From the measuring can, the motorist had to filter the gasoline through a chamois-lined funnel into the tank of the automobile. This smelly and messy process involved enough spillage and evaporation to be exceedingly dangerous.

Eventually, bargain hunters began to bypass the in-town

Fig. 1 Detroit, Michigan

4

Fig. 2   Refueling in 1901

Fig. 3   St. Louis, Missouri

retailers in favor of a trip directly to the wholesaler's bulk station. As they came in greater numbers, these drivers interfered with the bulk station's normal operations. At any given time, several dozen cars might be parked beneath the elevated tanks while their owners trudged back and forth, carrying sloshing cans of fuel. Meanwhile, tank wagons led by teams of horses would pass through the throngs of motorists. It took a hardy spirit to refuel a car.

As early as 1905, a more efficient method of refueling was introduced. The proprietor of the Automobile Gasoline Company of St. Louis, C. H. Laessig, stood an old hot-water heater on end, equipped it with a glass gauge, and attached a garden hose with faucet. By this simple action, Laessig had solved one of the technological problems of his time; he had invented a way to deliver gas directly from the storage tank to the automobile. This gravity-fed system eliminated the need for the gasoline-filled bucket. However, the driver still had to travel to the edge of town in order to refuel safely and economically. At the same time, another feature of the station as we have come to know it emerged.

The introduction of the gas pump is credited to Sylvanus F. Bowser. A man without formal education, he originally envisioned a simple pump as a pragmatic solution—a device to draw water from a well to protect his hands from the cold, icy bucket rope. Applying this principle initially to kerosene, in 1898 Bowser began building and marketing storage tanks outfitted with hand pumps. These pumps were easier to use than the traditional spigot and drum. The technique could be adopted by petroleum vendors—in existing grocery stores and other outlets—or by street vendors. The pump distribution was safer, less messy and wasteful, and had a self-measuring capability. More significant for those who added petroleum to their wares, these pumps in their waterproof cabinets could remain outside yet be locked at night. In 1905, the Bowser cabinet containing the pump assembly was labeled the "Filling Station."

The widespread use of pumps finally allowed the retail distribution of gasoline to become separated from the bulk station. Sheds with curbside pumps sprang up wherever auto-

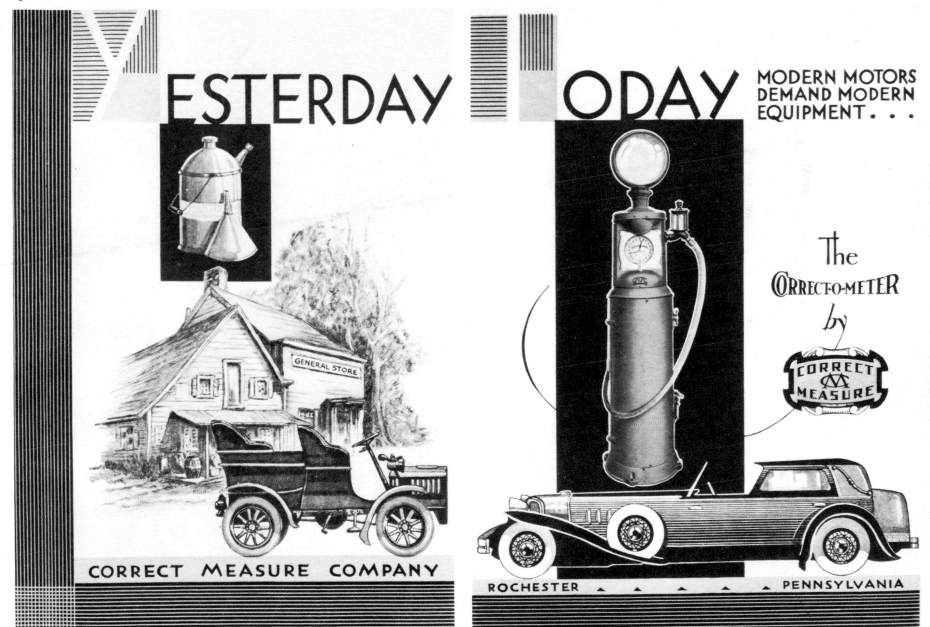

6

Fig. 6
Hartford,
Connecticut

Fig. 7
St. Louis,
Missouri

mobile traffic was heaviest. A new problem appeared, however: Streetside refueling caused serious traffic congestion. Lines of chugging, convulsing cars frightened horses and irritated pedestrians and other motorists. Once again, the Automobile Gasoline Company of St. Louis was among the first to offer a solution to an auto-age dilemma.

With its success in the bulk plant, the Automobile Gasoline Company decided to enter into direct gasoline distribution for cars. On an ordinary city lot, the company constructed a small brick building, paved the yard behind, and erected four gas pumps. These pumps, modifications of Bowser's devices, drew not from small, above-grade barrels but from safer, more advanced, underground tanks; they combined this convenience with Laessig's hose hook-ups, which funneled gasoline directly into the car. As a contemporary evaluation stated, "It takes but a few minutes to get in, fill the tank and get out again and the operation has cost the automobile owner anywhere from eight to ten cents a gallon less than if he went to a garage." This combination of features—modern pumps supplied by underground tanks, which fed directly to the auto; office building; paved, drive-through lot—was the prototype of the modern gas station, a drive-in store responding exclusively to the requirements of the automobile.

Station buildings of the 1910s usually stood on one corner of their broad paved lots. These simple brick or metal sheds served as office and storehouse, with convenience as their main virtue. Since the demand for gasoline exceeded the supply, the building did not need to project an image to attract customers.

Locating a station on a site where it would have maximum exposure to traffic wasn't easy. In the early part of the century, with few streets paved and the national highway system not yet established, roads often ended abruptly. Traffic patterns were constantly changing which made it difficult to decide where to build a gas station and hard to make a commitment to a site. Yet the petroleum retailers needed to establish themselves on these new roads as quickly as possible.

The solution? Prefabricated gas stations. Not only were these metal and glass structures portable but they could be erected and operating in a few days. Manufactured by several iron-works companies, these simple metal and glass buildings looked like a cross between an industrial shed and a greenhouse. Their steel structures offered all the advantages of fireproof masonry stations, at one-third the building cost.

Initially, in the teens, privately owned stores called "split-pump stations" sold several different brands of gasoline at one location. But then the breakup of John D. Rockefeller's Standard Oil trust in 1911, combined with a large number of new oil discoveries in the South and West, ushered in an

Fig. 8 Split-pump station, 1912

8

Fig. 9
Texaco
attendant

Fig. 10   Conoco attendant

unprecedented era of corporate rivalry. Oil men realized that new marketing strategies would be necessary in order to dominate other producers.

Since gasoline could not be judged on the basis of sight, taste, smell, or anything else within the ken of most motorists, corporate image became the principal mark that distinguished one brand from another. Brand loyalties had to be instilled among consumers. Companies adopted logos and slogans to differentiate their wares from those of the competition. "Visible pumps" appeared at this time. The gasoline flowed into a graduated cylinder atop the pump and then drained through a hose into the car's tank. The consumer could see the actual product and quantity being purchased. The now-visible gasoline was often dyed to distinguish brands and qualities of motor fuel. A sparkling clear gas dyed a royal purple, for instance, announced its high quality. Producers insisted upon controlling every stage in the life of their product, particularly the final stage of marketing. Gasoline wholesale marketers demanded that retailers affiliate exclusively with one brand.

The success of the drive-in gas station only fed the fierce competition among oil companies. To gain greater commercial advantage over one another, petroleum producers diversified the products and services offered at their gas stations. First motor oil and lubricants and then TBAs (tires, batteries, and accessories) evolved into a standard part of the inventory of most stations. Courtesy services such as engine cranking (in the early days), windshield wiping, and oil checks were instituted to promote goodwill and increase sales.

Adding pits and lifts for car maintenance and repair further encouraged motorists to view the gas station as an alternative to the repair shop. Though first built outdoors adjacent to the station proper, pits and lifts were eventually enclosed by extensions of the main structure. The lubritorium, as it came to be known, developed into a year-round, all-weather maintenance building that was an integral part of the gas station.

These changes in function required modification of the

station's design. Display windows—be they quaint yet enlarged bay windows or sleek, ultramodern glass cases—and accessory showrooms expanded the station building's role from a mere attendant's shelter to a store with lavish exhibits of automotive products. The lubritorium, a large box adjacent to the attendant's shelter and showroom, often echoed the stylistic theme of the smaller building. It more than doubled the size of the basic gas station, making the whole structure more prominent.

By the end of the 1920s, the one-stop super-service station that we know today had become a roadside fixture. This station provided under one roof all the functions of gasoline distribution and normal automotive maintenance.

Despite the many changes in gasoline marketing in the last fifty years, there have been no new gasoline distribution methods. In fact, today's stations are in many ways reintroductions of station types that existed before 1930. The full-service gas station corresponds to the old-fashioned repair shop that sold gasoline; the contemporary self-service station calls to mind the early bulk station; and the modern convenience store, with gasoline pumps, directly parallels the dry goods store that sold gasoline. Today's most advanced petroleum distribution methods are actually time-tested techniques. We have come full circle.

World War I dramatized the need for a comprehensive, well-planned network of national roads. The resulting highway construction boom of the 1920s laid roads through once isolated areas in order to connect neighboring towns. Since gasoline distribution was no longer tied to the local retailer or bulk plant, stations could locate anywhere that business existed. As travel increased, gasoline stations punctuated long stretches of the open road. In order to convince the new breed of traveler that their products were of uniform quality and reliability, petroleum companies began to standardize their affiliate stations.

The companies began to offer amenities for the motorist and his passengers, as well as fuel for the car itself. Previously an extra convenience, gas station restrooms became a

Fig. 11 Sunoco lubritorium

requirement. Often lavishly appointed, these restrooms in urban areas provided attendants, an amenity more often associated with luxurious hotels and restaurants. In rural stations, Texaco, for example, began a program in the 1930s featuring uniformly clean "registered" restrooms. Companies provided free road maps that often located their associated stations. As travel for pleasure became common, stations offered soft drinks, snacks, and tobacco to serve the weary voyager. Some stations attracted several other businesses: diners, tourist courts, and auto camps, all catering to the motorist. Though few at the time recognized it, the gas station was rapidly becoming the nucleus of the drive-in culture.

Despite the thrill of automobile travel, fear of the unknown colored long-distance trips. Petroleum companies

Fig. 12 Detroit, Michigan

Fig. 13   Houston, Texas

Fig. 14 Onondaga, New York

Fig. 15 Houston, Texas

Fig. 16
Free road map at
1934 Gulf station

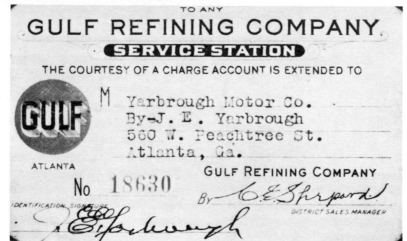

Fig. 17
1930s Gulf
credit card

standardized their affiliate stations so that they would be a familiar sight in an otherwise unfamiliar landscape. Station attendants in uniforms reinforced the desired familiar atmosphere and bestowed an air of legitimacy and authority on gas station personnel. Customers preferred dealing with a uniformed representative of a trusted company rather than a total stranger. "You can trust your car to the man who wears the star," the Texaco slogan ran.

The uniquely American concept of a credit card system had its beginnings as a gasoline purchasing convenience. Intended to make credit as mobile as the consumer, this system was modeled on an ordinary charge account at any local store. Gasoline companies issued identifying cards to their customers, thus enabling them to obtain gas and automotive accessories at any location. In every way, the oil companies sought to create in their affiliates the illusion of "your neighborhood station away from home."

The gas station building itself was the largest packaging device available to gasoline marketers. As a three-dimensional billboard, the gas station certainly gained attention; when repeated across the countryside, it acquired extra sales value. The carefully designed station multiplied the worth of every word of printed advertising and became a fundamental part of the entire merchandising effort. A distinctly standardized design could, in any setting, be synonymous with a particular brand of gasoline.

In its communication with the motorist, the most important function the gas station performs is conveying an image. These images fall into a series of recurring themes that have appeared in gas station design: Over time, *Fantastic* stations have appealed to the motorist's desire for adventure or novelty, *Respectable* stations to his sense of dignity, *Domestic* stations to his need for familiarity, and "*Functional*" stations to his sense of efficiency. Styles of gas stations have clearly come to reflect larger aspects of America's growing drive-in culture. Just as he views his new car as more than a simple conveyance, so the driver may see his local station as more than just a building with gas pumps.

By the mid-1920s, filling stations were beginning to dot our landscape but the building type remained a novelty. There was no precedent, no fixed idea of what the station should look like. Clearly, however, to attract the motorist, stations had to do more than just supply gas; they had to catch his eye. This led some designers, often petroleum retailers themselves, to dream up fanciful, dramatic station structures. Airplanes, boats, petroleum containers, icebergs, pyramids, and pagodas were among the inspirations for station design. These buildings were among the first to face the problem of packaging: projecting a unique image, quickly identifiable to the motorist as he speeded past.

During the "Roaring Twenties," the generation home from World War I took to the road in droves, flaunting their new mobility and prosperity. The war had destroyed many social barriers. Women were voting, smoking, wearing bobbed hair, and drinking with their boyfriends in the rumble seats of their Stutz Bearcats. Equally astounding technological advances, paralleling these social changes, occurred during this time. The war effort accelerated aviation technology to five times what it had been during peacetime. In 1927, Charles Lindbergh completed the first nonstop solo flight from New York to Paris, then came home to ticker-tape parades, banner headlines, and a hero's welcome in small towns across America. The public's romance with his journey was not lost on gas station designers. The overwhelming response to Lindbergh's expedition was a reflection of how deeply enthralled the world was with the magic of flight. Any number of stations took the form of single-propeller airplanes, with the "fuselage" serving as office and the "wings" as service canopies. More recent stations feature the hulks of old airplanes perched above their simple gas station buildings. Such stations implied a glamorous correspondence between the adventuresome traveler of the skies and the earthbound explorer of the American landscape.

Contrasting with this advanced air travel, a station constructed in 1929 near Atlantic City took the form of a galleon. It suggested the world of adventurous exploration, as well as

Fig. 18   Gulf honors the "Spirit of St. Louis"

Fig. 19 Huntington, New York

Fig. 20 Miami Beach, Florida

the more immediate pleasures available to the traveler at the seaside resort.

Continuing the nautical imagery along the East Coast were stations modeled after lighthouses, replete with flashing beacons that not only lent authenticity to the structure but also attracted the motorist's attention from a distance. Lighthouse stations appeared in a variety of forms ranging from modest two-pump models to stations that provided a host of other services.

A landmark to highway voyagers on the road to the seaside resort of Montauk, New York, was a Socony (Mobil) "lighthouse." In 1933 this station was awarded a prize for contributing to the "protection of natural scenic and roadside beauty of Long Island" by the roadside committee of the local chamber of commerce.

Appropriately situated at the entrance to Miami Beach on Biscayne Bay was a lighthouse station that catered to automobiles as well as boats. The tower with its light was not merely a beacon; it housed the fishing fleet's radio room as well. The complex also included a small hotel, restaurant, tackle shop, and parking lot. This establishment, in operation by the late 1930s, was perhaps the most elaborately executed lighthouse station.

In the 1960s, the possibilities of space travel opened a "new frontier" in gas station design. What could be more appropriate for the refueling of a Rocket Action Oldsmobile than a gas station resembling its futuristic counterpart, the space station? The radiating, futuristic forms of Gulf's recent "space" station in Atlanta suggest not only romantic travel but also advanced technology, effectively creating a station with a truly fantastic ambience.

Fig. 21   1960s Sinclair Dino gas pump

Before gasoline was measured directly by the metered pump, one had to draw it out of a tank and purchase it by the volume measure. Even after the introduction of the gas pump, motor oil continued for many years to be drawn out of a bulk tank and sold by the standard measure. The measuring can, with its distinctive appearance, became a suitable object to be replicated as a building selling gasoline. Such a station, appropriately named the Gallon Measure Service Station, opened in 1929 in Buchanan, New York. The white, cylindrical concrete building formed the container, while a chimney in the rear served as a "handle," and a pressed metal coping over the door created the "spout." The upper portion

of the container served as a sleeping loft for attendants on the night shift.

Rather than mimic a flamboyant transportation conveyance, whimsical stations of this type transformed their buildings into outsized versions of elements of the automobile culture. These stations, such as a New England station of the late 1920s in the form of a large gas pump, served as signs proclaiming their function.

A contemporary Houston, Texas, structure takes the shape of a gas can used for emergency highway refueling. It even sports a "spout" and "screw-on" lid. This form serves to reinforce graphically the message conveyed by a small sign that reads: Last Gas Before Freeway.

Touted as "as nearly an exact replica of a tank car as it is possible to make a service station" is a Creston, Iowa, station that opened in 1930. This outlet heightened its realism by having wheels painted on the building's sides. This inventive design (which was repeated in a series of adjacent tourist cabins) referred to the delivery methods of gasoline, as well as to the open-air bulk stations of the past.

Reflecting the origin of petroleum in its crudest form is a station made to look like an oil derrick in Matador, Texas. Station design sometimes portrayed other less honest aspects of the petroleum industry. In Zillah, Washington, a 1923 station modeled after a teapot commemorated the Teapot Dome scandal in which the rich naval oil reserves of Teapot Dome, Wyoming, and Elk Hills, California, were surreptitiously leased to private entrepreneurs for personal exploitation.

As brand-name awareness increased among motorists during the 1930s, some station owners capitalized on corporate imagery to convey the merits of their specific products. A Shell station of this era was a giant concrete reproduction of the company logo. The eighteen-foot-high shell displayed a shape so familiar to most drivers that the station's function was immediately apparent. The form may have been inspired by the highly publicized five-story shell-shaped travel and tourist pavilion at the California Pacific International Exposition of 1936. One of eight of a local retailer's chain in the

Fig. 22 Atlanta, Georgia

Fig. 24
Winston-Salem,
North Carolina

Winston-Salem area, this building is a splendid example of the naïve literalism that characterized many roadside buildings of the late 1920s and 1930s. Like the Sinclair Oil Company's remarkable "Dino" station, which was a concrete embodiment of Dino the Dinosaur, the company's lovable mascot-logo, these stations formed an important phase not only in early gas station design but in the increasingly important auto-oriented commercial architecture as well. Despite their small size and whimsical nature, these structures were the first to deal with the serious issue of an architecture of communication in a changing motor age.

Fig. 23 Buchanan, New York

In the twenties and thirties, the world of adventure and exploration made possible by the automobile provided yet another theme for gas station designs. Numerous stations of these decades celebrated the attractions awaiting the new breed of tourist as he traveled America's highways. Taking as their subject natural formations, regional curiosities, and cultural differences, these stations attracted customers while making only slight reference to the products they sold.

The "natural wonders" stations invited tourists to refuel and sightsee at the same time. Postcards and souvenirs proclaimed a Colorado station to be the "Only Petrified Wood Filling Station." A South Dakota station was part of the "World's Largest Petrified Wood Park," a tourist attraction consisting of 3,200 tons of petrified wood cemented together to form conical pyramids, pillars, and other unusual shapes. In Ukiah, California, a station was built in the trunk of a hollowed-out redwood tree and billed as the "World's Largest Redwood Tree Service Station."

Fig. 25
San Antonio,
Texas

A San Antonio, Texas, station from the late 1920s features tree-trunk canopies over its pumps. Although the entire structure is actually built of concrete, every detail has been presented to give the appearance of natural tree limbs. Painstaking attention is lavished on every embellishment, including knotholes and protruding, twiglike branches. (This station echoes the theme from the city's nearby Brackenridge Park, a tourist attraction featuring similar concrete formations.)

It took a family of highway contractors a number of years to amass the materials for their "natural wonder" station and motel. Located south of San Luis Obispo, California, a carefully crafted assemblage of enormous boulders forms a motel and gas station. In 1967 architect Charles Moore termed his visit to the Madonna Inn as "exhilarating . . . one of the most surprisingly full experiences to be found along the American highway."

Chances are that if the terrain did not provide a local wonder, one could be created—particularly if something incongruous enough to be eye-catching could be devised.

Giant icebergs, the only interruption looming on flat, arid terrain, might be visible to the motorist for miles. The prairies of Ottawa, Kansas, and Albuquerque, New Mexico, were settings for two such stations. The "iceberg" communicated to the motorist the promise of a refreshing respite from his travels.

A combination eatery–filling station in the form of a southern mammy located on US Highway 61 in Mississippi recalls the images of traditional southern hospitality in an area known for its often-toured antebellum mansions. In addition to gasoline, the engaging mammy figure offers, beneath her billowing brick skirts, pancakes and other southern fare. Just as the mammy reflects the heritage of its location, other stations also echo local culture. The Headless Horseman Texaco station stands in Tarrytown, New York, within a short distance of the site of Ichabod Crane's legendary ride. The station, which was converted from an inn in 1929, appears from a distance to be a full-sized structure. Its name

recalls Washington Irving's famous story, and its size, smaller than life, creates a storybook feeling (a concept later exploited by Walt Disney at Disneyland).

A Glen Elder, Kansas, station of 1926 calls to mind a thoroughly defensible medieval castle. Composed entirely of local buff-colored limestone, this station featured four battlements, each of which had crenellated turrets spanning a shallow-arched canopy that extended over the service drive. Its two front towers served as booths for the attendants. Although fantastic in appearance, the station's design was based upon the owner's sketches of a castle he saw in Germany during World War I.

Fig. 26   Natchez, Mississippi

Fig. 27   Glen Elder, Kansas

Fig. 28 Bardstown, Kentucky

A station-cabin camp complex near Bardstown, Kentucky, invited motorists to "Eat and Sleep in a Wigwam." Throughout the late twenties and early thirties the teepee form was adopted, often expanding into an adjoining motor court. The teepee had an exotic and mystical quality that gave these structures an aura of adventure and excitement. A premier example of the wigwam phenomenon opened near Lawrence, Kansas, in 1930. The plans for the complex included a fifty-foot-tall "teepee" station to stand in front of fourteen smaller, similarly shaped tourist cabins arranged in a semicircular pattern in, as a contemporary appraisal put it, "True Indian Fashion." Allegorical Indian paintings adorned these buildings, which were made of buckskin-colored stucco and had poles jutting from their tops. A teepee-shaped curio shop, barbecue stand, and utility building completed the theme. The station's attendants, who were Indians dressed in the ancestral garb of their various tribes, reinforced the authentic atmosphere.

The windmill, a structure often associated with a foreign culture, easily lent itself to conversion into an especially practical filling station. Like the lighthouse, the windmill form, small but visually prominent, was well suited to the advertising needs of station owners. Large rotating blades served as signboards that would easily gain the notice of the driver. Sometimes each blade announced, in illuminated letters, a function: gas, oil, grease, and service.

Between 1925 and 1930 a series of stations built by individual retailers appeared in the form of windmills. Typical of the period, they were often combined with restaurants and cabin camps. Although they were built throughout the country, windmills usually appeared in regions with a sizable Dutch population or a link with Dutch culture. Among the locations were: Holland, Michigan; Schenectady, New York (founded by the Dutch in 1675); Macomb, Illinois; and throughout Iowa and Pennsylvania Dutch country. An Iowa retailer, using the name Dutch Mill Service Company, opened a series of five blue and white Dutch windmill stations in southern Iowa. Perhaps the retailer's proximity to Pella,

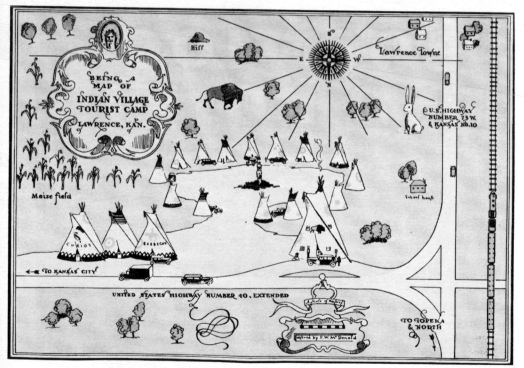

Fig. 29 Map of tourist camp—gas station, Lawrence, Kansas

Fig. 30   Albia, Iowa

Iowa's premier Dutch-American community, influenced his choice of an architectural motif. The use of the windmill form created a series of distinctive stations.

The architecture of foreign cultures found even more elaborate expression in stations throughout the country during the twenties and thirties. Their appeal derived from their being exotic and completely unexpected; they intrigued the motorist because they juxtaposed a foreign image with the familiar American countryside. The pyramids of Egypt inspired a series of stations in Maine. Their owner and developer, Donald Abbot, constructed the chain in 1932. Abbot named his tiny domain Oasis, Incorporated, and chose as his slogan, "Where a Thirsty Engine Gets a Drink." The station buildings were wood-frame pyramids, flanked on either side by smaller pyramids, which served as restrooms. All the decorative features reflected the pyramid motif. Trees and shrubs surrounding the site were trimmed to pyramidal shape. Even the light standards and fence echoed the triangular forms.

Stations with foreign themes romanticized travel and often became identified in the customer's mind with a particular retailer's products. Oriental architecture was the inspiration for many especially attractive exotic gas stations. Perhaps the best-known example of a company making this architectural motif synonymous with its name was the Wadham's Oil and Grease Company of Wisconsin. In 1916 the company retained Alexander C. Eschweiler, a prominent Milwaukee society architect known for his period-revival designs. The company's president instructed Eschweiler to develop a station that would meet a few basic criteria: The prototype should be of an unusual design that would become immediately recognizable as a Wadham's station; it should be inexpensive to build; and it must be portable so that it could be moved to conform to changing patterns of trade.

Eschweiler was accustomed to designing in given architectural idioms. Without an appropriate style to employ for this new building type, he turned to the Orient for his model. Though unprecedented, his choice was far less eccentric

Fig. 31   Milwaukee, Wisconsin

Fig. 32 Los Angeles, California

than it may at first seem. Oriental and especially Japanese architecture had appeared throughout the Midwest for at least twenty-five years by 1916. Japanese displays had been highly influential showpieces at the Chicago World's Columbian Exposition in 1893 and at the Louisiana Purchase Exposition in St. Louis in 1904. The work and writings of well-known architects such as Ralph Adams Cram and Frank Lloyd Wright had introduced a generation of designers to the oriental tradition. From a purely practical standpoint, Eschweiler must have taken into account that a small yet distinctive building of this mode could become uniquely associated with one brand of gas. In addition, the oriental tradition of impermanence in building would be appropriate for the portability that his client requested.

The first station based on Eschweiler's prototype was built in Milwaukee in 1917. This structure, like the others that followed, featured a characteristic swooping oriental roof. The first stations were brightly painted in the company colors of red, black, and yellow. At its most elaborate, the station bore a multitiered pagodalike appurtenance; several included stained-glass Ws beneath the gabled ends of their ornate roofs. Small, swooping roofs topped the gas pumps' clear glass globes. The Wadham's "oriental" station proved immensely popular and successful, and between 1917 and 1930 over a hundred were built.

Distinctive in appearance, "oriental" stations abounded throughout the twenties and thirties. Often this motif was combined with more traditional architectural elements. In Dayton, Ohio, a Power Plus station in operation by 1923 was capped by a light oriental-style roof, which rested, however, on massive stone piers. These projected an equally exotic flavor: Their battered forms suggested the Egyptian while their massive stonework evoked the Romanesque. A Mobile, Alabama, station built for the Huxford Oil Company in 1926 featured sweeping oriental-roofed canopies, supported by enlarged, almost classical console brackets. Those, combined with the Victorian spindle-work, contradicted the oriental imagery. But what passing motorist would notice anything other than the station's principal oriental theme?

The popularity of this style led to the production of prefabricated oriental-style stations during the 1920s. Oriental roofs extended dramatically beyond the actual small buildings to shelter their driveways. Extensive oriental ornamentation around the station's windows and doors reinforced the foreign imagery.

The oriental vocabulary was sometimes employed in an effort to blend stations into an existing oriental community. Accordingly, about 1930, an "oriental" Texaco station emerged at the Mandarin Market in Hollywood, "Where the Bizarre Is Usual," and another cropped up recently under the Chevron trademark in San Francisco's Chinatown.

Like Alexander Eschweiler, Roland E. Coate was a respected period-revival architect, based in California. When faced with the issue of filling station design, he veered from the accepted Mediterranean Revival to create a flamboyant stucco and tile composition reminiscent of an Islamic mosque. One of his more lavish stations, designed for the California Petroleum Corporation (Calpet), opened on Los Angeles's fashionable Wilshire Boulevard in 1927. A central domed kiosk with lateral drive-through wings housing the pumps dominated the station. Red, yellow, and black Tunis tiles accentuated the white stucco building's base, its trim, and the four-sided dome over the kiosk. The entire grounds of the complex were paved in red concrete and contained plantings that underscored the Islamic theme. The station's lavish exterior paralleled the luxurious interior, offering its patrons a venetian mirror, marble-topped tables, wicker settees, chandeliers, as well as a carpeted smoking room. The Calpet station's lush decor and elegant design made it an appropriate symbol of the Beverly Hills life-style during the thirties.

Byzantine fantasies did not go unrepresented in station design. In Washington, DC, in the mid-1920s, Horace Peaslee designed such a station for the Columbia Oil Company. An octagonal, unadorned stucco structure, its central drum topped with a row of small, round windows, rises above the semicircular side wings. Each element was capped by gently sloping tile roofs. The station conveys the image of the monuments of early Christian architecture, as epitomized by the

Fig. 33
Washington, DC

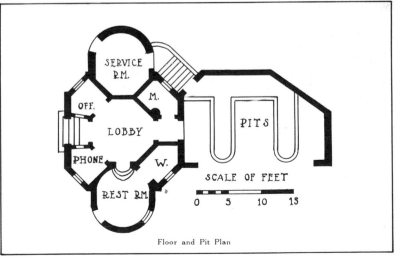

Floor and Pit Plan

famous Byzantine Church San Vitale in Ravenna. The building form was well adapted to its function. The roof's overhanging eaves concealed electric bulbs that dramatically flooded the building's walls with light at night. The plan of the building, with its central office, made use of the composition's symmetry in creating a practical arrangement.

Like other Fantastic stations, this design re-created the forms of an architecture that had little direct influence upon American building and projected a foreign, incongruous image that piqued the driver's curiosity. While sharing these attributes with other stations of this group, the Columbia station's esoteric theme distinguished it from the eccentricity of the mammy station, and even from the more conventional yet exotic "oriental" stations. Peaslee's design to some extent elicits the motorist's respect as well as his curiosity and his sense of adventure. The idea that a filling station might be taken seriously—indeed, that it might be an architectural asset to the community—was a widespread belief that underlies a different but equally colorful chapter in the stations' history.

Between 1920 and 1935, the Fantastic experienced its golden age. After 1930, the consolidation of the larger oil companies, the involvement of fewer independent operators, and the development of unified corporate marketing techniques all contributed to the decline of the Fantastic gas station.

The Respectable 3

During the 1920s, petroleum retailers strove to legitimize the gas station in general and their specific merchandise in particular. Respectable stations, like the Fantastic ones, attempted to catch the eye of passing motorists. Rather than appealing to curiosity, however, these stations created an aura of prestige and grandeur. Capturing the flavor of buildings of great stature or civic importance, such as courthouses, banks, or university halls, these stations often stood as monuments to the institutions for which they were built. Designs establishing a link with romanticized notions of the past suggest, through the use of architectural elements and forms, revered American institutions and their lofty ideals and high values. Similarly, stations copying or directly emulating particularly prominent buildings attain respectability more directly. Respectable stations prompted stories and cartoons, such as one of a midwestern motorist, touring the East, who "came to a dead stop in front of Grant's Tomb and yelled 'fill 'er up' to the guard standing nearby."

The Respectable gas station sprang from a growing sentiment among urban reformers and design professionals that "the service station can be made a civic asset." At the turn of the century, critics saw the American urban scene taking an alarming turn, with cities fast becoming chaotic and ugly. The impetus for this awareness and civic concern is often linked to the Chicago World's Fair of 1893. The classical architecture of this "white city" featured white beaux arts palaces, reminiscent of ancient Rome and Renaissance Italy. The fair's representation of an idealized Europe by architects who had studied abroad, introduced Americans to a dazzling new concept of urban order associated with the fair's exuberant architecture.

The City Beautiful movement in America reflected the force of civic pride and concern for the quality of urban life. It sought to replace artless cityscapes with more idealized European urban scenes characterized by great boulevards, plazas, monuments, bridges, and esplanades. The concern for civic beauty, for the elimination of hideous signs and crass billboards in favor of trees, fountains, and statues formed the basis for the movement. By the late teens, the powerful City Beautiful movement linked civic beauty to a variety of concerns, ranging from the quality of life to moral values.

Advocates of civic reform often singled out gas stations as an example of urban blight. As the *American City* magazine, one of the publications promoting civic reform in the 1920s, pointed out, "Filling stations were not . . . matters of civic pride." Stating the same sentiments more forcefully, a later issue of the same journal declared, "Streets throughout the entire country are littered by horrible examples of poorly designed filling stations." Recognizing that the gas station had become an indispensable part of urban development, cities passed ordinances that governed the design and location of these buildings. Through regulation, it was hoped that a necessary evil could be turned into a pleasing addition, complementing the cityscape rather than standing out as an eyesore.

In response to the outcry for more dignified gas stations, some petroleum companies built small pavilion stations that appeared as monuments of civic beauty, embellishing the lavish urban boulevards so much a part of most City Beauti-

Fig. 34 1920s cartoon

ONE OF THE SIGHTS IN MOST ANY TOWN

In the early 1920s, a truly classical gem was erected in Philadelphia by the Atlantic Refining Company. A circular building on a raised platform surrounded by columns was declard by its designer to be "dedicated to the goddess of internal combustion" and was described as a "reproduction, on an enlarged scale, of the monument to Lysicrates in Athens." The pavilion, the architect continued, was "surrounded on two sides by an Ionic colonnade, the details of which are taken from the Erectheum." Hailed as a fine design, this station stood "in striking contrast to the great majority of buildings erected for the purpose of supplying the wants of modern charioteers."

Because of its direct derivation from an ancient Greek prototype, this building might appear more akin to the exotic Fantastic stations. Upon closer examination, however, the station reveals a more complicated stylistic ancestry. Linking it more directly to the Respectable, the Atlantic station also bears a marked similarity to William Strickland's famous Philadelphia Merchant's Exchange Building of 1832–34. The Exchange, located on the same street as the station, is itself a free reinterpretation of the monument to Lysicrates and typifies neoclassical design. Whatever the actual prototype, the station was built in a style that has come to be associated with respectable buildings. This pavilion, featuring elegant details and an elaborate symmetry, was one of a series of small stations creating a grand statement, although housing only a simple sales office. Subsidiary buildings housed other services, minimizing conflict with the main structure. The architecture of these stations ranged from strictly classical themes to the more elaborate exuberant beaux arts variations of classicism popularized by the Chicago World's Fair of 1893.

As these City Beautiful pavilion stations gained acceptance, prefabricated metal and glass buildings of this style began to be manufactured and distributed across the country. Classical motifs, including elaborate ornamented columns and pilasters, formed from pressed metal, decorated the buildings. The Edwards Manufacturing Company of Cin-

ful schemes. These elegant pavilions reflected the petroleum companies' interest in enhancing the cityscape rather than contributing to its desecration.

cinnati, Ohio, produced a prefabricated model that achieved great popularity. The Pure Oil Company purchased these in quantity and adopted them as their standardized station.

Small, neatly groomed gardens, bubbling fountains, and station paraphernalia, designed to double as the "street furniture" so much a part of civic concern, were all essential to the composition. Manufacturers of prefabricated buildings offered catalogues illustrating hundreds of available accessories. Classical columns (actually light standards) featured ornate bases and abbreviated capitals bearing light globes. Visible glass tanks topped fanciful Ionic columns, betraying their real function as gas pumps. When combined with the pavilion stations, these lavish accessories created an aura of dignity.

The Beacon Oil Company built several identical Respectable stations in the 1920s. Although still basically a pavilion, this design is such a well-executed tour de force that it gives the impression of being a monumental building. An imposing dome, emphasized by a heavy carved railing, caps the composition. Half the domical roof covers a small two-story office and restroom structure. The forward portion of the dome, supported by four colossal Corinthian columns, covers no building at all, but merely shelters the driveway, making it a well-integrated part of the station. Tucked under the dome, the façade of the office shelter contains a well-proportioned, carefully detailed doorway, flanked by classically detailed windows.

These domed Beacon stations recall Jefferson's University of Virginia at Charlottesville and his home, Monticello. They are also reminiscent of a myriad of prestigious public buildings that combine impressive architecture with a legacy of their own.

Just as the neoclassical theme provided the inspiration for respectable institutional buildings in the East and Northeast, sections of the West and Southwest were beginning to be graced with a number of important structures built in the Spanish mode. Although romantic imagination may have shaped much of this style, it had some historic precedent in

Fig. 35 Philadelphia, Pennsylvania

Fig. 36
Columbus,
Ohio

the architecture of the Spanish missions. By the 1930s, the style had become a popular idiom for important public and private buildings in Arizona, New Mexico, and California.

In 1927, the Union Oil Company of California sponsored a competition for the design of a "dignified oil-filling station." They received an overwhelming response of more than 100 entries. An elaborately rendered octagonal pavilion featuring plain white stucco walls captured first prize. A more conservative octagonal pavilion with a Spanish tile roof also received an award. None of the entries was built as submitted, but a combination of the features of these two award winners created a standard design for the Southwest. A small hexagonal structure resulted, which, with its smooth white stucco walls, tile roofs, and quatrefoil windows with wrought-iron grillwork, exhibited a distinctly Spanish flavor. The service island canopies and restroom pavilion repeated this motif. This station seems to represent the Southwest's coun-

Fig. 37   Dorchester, Massachusetts

Fig. 38
1930 Union
Oil Co.
prototype

terpart to the stately, more formal classical pavilions of the East.

In the 1920s, the destruction in Charleston, South Carolina, of the then 120-year-old Gabriel Manigault mansion, a fine example of colonial architecture, made available some key decorative elements that were transplanted and incorporated into the design of a local service station. Using the original bricks, the station creates an appropriate setting for these distinctive features, including finely crafted door and window trim and impressive Ionic columns. A colonial baluster caps the building. Although this station recycled its respectable elements from a locally significant mansion, many other simple stations, like one in Dorchester, Massachusetts, attached new, grand, decorative trim. A finely detailed colonial door graced with a dignified fanlight and sidelights, or with elegant colonial windows, a colonial balustrade, or a majestic Palladian window, lent respectability to

Fig. 39   Dorchester, Massachusetts

Fig. 40
Vincennes,
Indiana

a simple station. This ornamentation contributed a dignity that transcended the building's basic simplistic form.

As the boxlike filling station expanded to house more services under one roof, small, well-detailed trim, such as an elaborate doorway, would no longer suffice to give the large, more massive station an overall aura of prestige. A larger, more dominant element, like a grand pedimented portico supported by tall, elegant columns, left the imprint of respectability yet often served a practical function as well. The portico sheltered the service drives for refueling cars while creating a focal point for the large rambling station. Often a clock was placed in the pediment, emphasizing the link with Respectable buildings, such as banks and churches, built in this style. From the porticos' ceilings hung majestic lanterns illuminating the driveway.

Stations in the Southwest also employed the single large element to give a focus and a sense of order to their designs.

Fig. 41   Oklahoma City, Oklahoma

Fig. 42
San Juan
Capistrano,
California

The "Spanish" counterpart to the classical porch might be a
portico that terminated in an elaborate gable, supported by
ornate clustered columns. Another motif associated with
Spanish colonial architecture also appeared in a number of
stations as a focal point. The bell tower, composed of a series
of receding squares topped by a low dome, achieved two
goals at once. Projecting vertically into space, the bell tower
gave the station visibility from a distance; at the same time,
it suggested a relationship with ecclesiastical architecture.

Porticos and bell towers have been used to give both stylistic distinction and focus to gas stations. Often these elements gave the appearance of being tacked on to a station
that otherwise made only minimal reference to these elaborate appendages. Sometimes they became so important that
they overshadowed the station structure itself.

Envisioned as service centers located every fifty miles
along the Pacific coast's highways from Canada to Mexico

Fig. 43 San Antonio, Texas

was a chain of Richfield outlets, each to be constructed in a mode reflective of the region's "native architecture." The 1928 station designed for the San Juan Capistrano site uses the Spanish motif to combine three discrete units. The building, with smooth stucco walls and Spanish tile roofs, displays a basic symmetry. The wings on either side of the central office create a unified appearance but are distinguished from each other by different wall openings. The station's three components—porch, office, and utility area—have been combined to create a pleasing whole.

A central pavilion, or pergola, flanked by two elaborate wings, creates a similar hacienda-style station in San Antonio, Texas. People could use the restrooms and feel they were entering an elegant hacienda. Another wing encloses the service bays, hidden away to avoid disturbing the elegant front. The central pergola houses the office. The building's wings retain their autonomy while creating a unified, respectable structure. In both of these stations, the more relaxed nature of Spanish architecture lends itself well to the construction of smoothly integrated buildings.

Built in 1936, a Gulf station in Washington, DC, employs finely detailed windows and roof forms to suggest a classical theme. A flat pediment, which merely serves a stylistic purpose, has come to replace the lavish portico of earlier stations. The sparing use of ornamentation suggests a type of civic architecture that emerged in Depression-era public works projects such as libraries, schools, and museums.

During the late thirties and early forties, Gulf and other companies created standardized designs that sported fewer details than their earlier counterparts. As motorists traveled at greater speeds, they would be more likely to notice larger, more straightforward features than to appreciate fine embellishments. Well integrated into these compositions, the colonial lantern or cupola was often employed as a station's most prominent element. No longer obscuring the building (as the bell tower or the portico had), it served double duty as an attention-attracting device and as a symbol of respectability.

Fig. 44 Cambridge, Massachusetts

During the forties, the acceptance of the modern movement in architecture eclipsed the use of historical styles. Classical motifs recalling the glorious past fell out of vogue. Straightforward, no-nonsense designs reflecting a more "functional" aesthetic emerged to dominate the architectural scene. Respectable service stations of the last twenty-five years, reverting to a more functional box, drastically reduced their ornamentation to a few vestigial elements. The cupola has been reduced to an abstraction, and the pediment is implied by simple woodwork attached directly to the box. Unlike their exquisitely detailed ancestors, the recent Respectable stations refer only subtly to dignified architectural forms, creating scaled-down versions of the earlier gleaming, lavish monuments.

Fig. 45
Pittsburgh,
Pennsylvania

Fig. 46 Palo Alto, California

Achieving an aura of prestige in a direct manner are stations that copy a specific prominent building. A Shell station designed in 1932 for a site opposite the Stanford University campus in Palo Alto, California, incorporated Romanesque details similar to those of the university's buildings. The design skillfully integrated the Shell logo with lavish florid carvings. Similarly, a station in Princeton, New Jersey, offering Gulf products echoed the neighboring university's collegiate Gothic forms. An impressive stone structure, the little building featured a large Gothic window and a steeply pitched slate roof. Not only were these stations in harmony with their surroundings but, more significantly, they borrowed the dignity associated with their academic neighbors for the purpose of marketing gasoline.

Rather than mimic an adjoining landmark, the Sherman Oaks service station in Van Nuys, California, copied the Los Angeles City Hall, with its soaring, stepped tower, capped by a pyramidal roof. The station reproduces precisely each section of the city hall's tower but adapts the base of the hall to form the gas station's covered driveway.

Like the grand old railroad stations or elaborate hotels of the last century, the airport has unusual civic status as a city's gateway. The flamboyant Gulf station at Atlanta's Hartsfield International Airport repeats the terminal's tent-like forms in both its building and driveway canopies. The prestige of Houston's Astrodome, locally considered the "eighth wonder of the world," is borrowed, although simplified and scaled down, by Texaco's adjacent gas station. Pittsburgh's Three Rivers Gulf station likewise duplicates the forms and colors of the Pirates' home stadium. The emulation of airport terminals or athletic stadiums rather than more traditional civic monuments reflects the broad range of institutions that have come to be considered respectable.

Under certain circumstances, the gas station achieved legitimacy not by adopting architectural motifs of other historic or contemporary buildings but by copying its own corporate edifices in miniature. A series of stations built in the thirties in California reproduced portions of the highly popu-

Fig. 47 (Detail) Palo Alto, California

Fig. 48 Van Nuys, California

Fig. 49   Houston, Texas

lar San Francisco headquarters of the Shell Oil Company. The company felt this building, a twenty-nine-story, buff-colored skyscraper designed by the architectural firm of George W. Kelhorn in 1930, had prompted such favorable public response that it could become a direct marketing asset. One of the project's designers, Herbert O. Alden, translated the architectural themes of the office structure into a series of stations. All of the designs displayed the tall, fluted columns of the office tower, but in other respects each one varied, taking as its theme one or another of the headquarters's stylistic details. A station in San Francisco, for example, restated in miniature a single section of the skyscraper's crowning tower.

Figs. 50 & 51 San Francisco, California

The Respectable station has, with time, changed its appearance a great deal. The early ornate beaux arts and classical extravaganzas, built with the idea of shaping American cities by force of will into an idealized, pristine image, embodies one notion of respectability. As the drive-in culture developed, respectability remained a viable theme, but the methods used to create a sense of dignity changed dramatically. The addition of stately embellishments—first finely detailed ornaments and then impressive large forms—rendered a station respectable. These additions to the simple boxlike buildings were, to varying degrees, integrated into the overall design. Throughout this time, some Respectable stations imitated specific noteworthy buildings. These more often complemented a particular setting rather than displaying general symbols of architectural prestige. In another category of station design, the Domestic, this notion of integrating a station with its setting is carried to its logical conclusion.

Fig. 52
Houston, Texas

During the late sixties, Gulf built a station adjacent to its new headquarters in Houston. Part of the corporate complex, this station echoes the forms of its parent company's nearby office building. An Exxon Car Care Center, also in Houston, borrows the theme of the corporation's nearby production research office to form the basis of its design. The trend to reproduce the architecture of corporate buildings in the company's service stations suggests the extent to which large corporations themselves have become established as respectable modern institutions.

Just as Respectable stations recalled America's dignified institutions, Domestic stations gained acceptance by adopting the appearance of houses, suggesting a link with perhaps America's most revered institution: the family. Unlike either Respectable or Fantastic stations, though, Domestic stations were neither imposing nor adventuresome. Instead, they conjured up warmer, more relaxed associations, suggesting the security and intimacy of "hearth and home." These stations were attractive not only to community residents but also to the traveler in a strange territory.

As concern for "good taste" and for the uniform appearance of cities as well as communities grew, the control of gas station design became an issue. Referring to both the Fantastic and Respectable stations, a 1925 *House and Garden* article stated, "If they were once too weird, they are now apt to be too elegant. Either weird or elegant, they strike a jarring note in their surroundings and stand, not as a monument to an enormous and vital industry, but to bad taste." The Domestic stations, usually based on popular suburban styles, offered the advantages of minimizing community opposition by not being in conflict with the buildings in their neighborhood. Gas stations projecting this image contradicted the machine age they signified, just as the suburb, also dependent on the automobile, denied the complexities of urban life.

A model for these idyllic stations was the Picturesque rustic cottage. The Picturesque movement had gained considerable popularity in England in the nineteenth century. Traditionally rural in orientation, it was much like the civic awareness that came over this country a century later in its almost evangelical drive to improve the quality of life by offering an alternative to the "poor taste" that was invading the English countryside. Theorists issued books with lavishly rendered drawings providing a variety of alternative styles for the rural buildings. Their illustrations featured pleasant groupings of buildings notable for their small scale, irregular silhouettes, and generally quaint quality. P. F. Robinson, a prominent architect and advocate of Picturesque principles, stated in one of his publications: "In the most beautiful parts of this country, the scenery is disfigured by the impotent attempts of the workman unaided by the pencil of the artist." It seems appropriate that a century later the effort in the United States to bring "good taste" to gasoline stations resulted in the adoption of this same theme.

Largely in response to the demand for "tasteful" filling stations, dozens of rural cottage models appeared during the twenties; they bore the clear stamp of the Picturesque influence. A Wisconsin station built in 1925 is typical. Irregularly laid, multitoned shingles covered the prominent, spectacularly swooping roofs. A deliberately uneven roof line, seeming to have sagged with age, complemented the rustic theme. The overhanging eaves hid the floodlights that dramatically illuminated the stucco and brick walls, which featured half-timbering. This station had shuttered windows and a large chimney from which the roof was spotlighted. The fanciful adaptation of the traditional weathervane in the form of an automobile being refueled added a touch of whimsy. As a contemporary description of this pleasing structure noted: "No one passing at less than forty miles an hour [a rapid speed for those days] could fail to notice this unusual bit of architecture." The characteristically irregular forms of

Fig. 53 Waupun, Wisconsin

these gas stations made them acceptable additions to their communities, yet caught the eye of the motorist.

To avoid detracting from the quaint atmosphere of such stations, petroleum pumps and other technical fixtures were either hidden behind the cottage or camouflaged as an element central to the Picturesque village: the water well.

The Pure Oil Company pioneered the standardization of the Domestic station. These stations bore all the rustic cottage's features, yet adapted them to the needs of corporate advertising. Although the cottage retained a steeply pitched roof, it was simplified, having no intersecting roof planes or uneven ridge pole. Shingled with regularly laid "Pure Oil blue" roof tiles, the roof attracts attention while conveying a corporate identity. In the front, a main bay window (enlarged for the display of products) offsets an arched doorway with a residential stoop and a tiny shuttered window adorned by a flower box. Shuttered windows and a garden trellis highlight the building's other sides. The trim repeats the standardized blue of the roof tiles, tying the entire composition together, illustrating, as one commentator put it, "how brands may be brought to the attention of the motorist without detracting from the orderly appearance of the station."

The Sun Oil Company also produced a series of Domestic stations even simpler and more symmetrical than the Pure Oil models. This design enjoyed unusual longevity, serving as a standard prototype from 1920 well into the thirties. Again, a tiled roof, this time featuring a curved window, most clearly expressed the building's theme. As in the Pure Oil station, both the shingles and the trim have been painted in company colors to remind the motorist of the brand and to unify the station's design. With its roof, trellises, and shrubbery, the Sun Oil station projected unmistakable domestic imagery. When this prototype was first developed, all the services were hidden from sight in back of the cottage. Only later did they come into view.

The addition of open-air grease pits and racks as well as equipment for cleaning cars posed a problem in Domestic station design. They were difficult to keep clean and present-

Fig. 54 Manitowoc, Wisconsin

Fig. 55 Binghamton, New York

44

Fig. 56
Philadelphia,
Pennsylvania

Fig. 57
Minneapolis,
Minnesota

able, and their presence conflicted with the domestic imagery. One solution involved hiding these services behind the stations, another housed them in adjacent buildings. These structures, ranging from plain sheds to elaborately decorated buildings, reinforced the station's ambience. Carrying the quest for stylistic uniformity to an amusing extreme, the Whitehall filling station in Kansas City, Missouri, consisted of a series of individual rustic cottages, each having its own function: washing, lubrication, and sales office. Together these formed an ensemble that resembled the idealized villages or hamlets so beautifully rendered in the frontispieces of nineteenth-century Picturesque handbooks.

Other stations had service wings of different shapes and sizes added to the existing cottages. A maintenance rack required a tall building; the washing area, a lower one. In the hands of a resourceful designer, the addition of irregularly shaped buildings to a simple cottage station might create the intersecting roof line, odd angles, and forms so typical of the Picturesque style. Far from looking unpleasantly tacked on, new service areas, often flanking the original cottage, enhanced the early Domestic stations.

By the thirties, accommodation of a variety of services was an integral part of station design. The super-service station often assumed the look of Tudor stables. These structures' L- or V-shaped layouts minimized the buildings' massiveness while defining their own "courtyards." (One can almost imagine horses being exercised and groomed in these courts.) Many of the details of the early rustic cottage stations—such as half-timbering with stucco, brick, and/or stone, as well as massive gabled roofs—reappeared. These elaborate structures contained, in addition to restrooms, enclosed service areas, an attendant's office, lounges, and covered porches from which customers could watch their cars being serviced, and elaborate showrooms for the sale of tires, batteries, and accessories.

Tudor super-service stations might have been small-scale imitations of country estates but, ironically, they rarely appeared in the country. Because they represented major investments, they required a large clientele that only a city or well-populated suburb could supply.

During the late 1920s and early 1930s, the growing popularity and availability of the automobile spurred the establishment of suburban communities, offering proximity to the city and reflecting the nostalgia for small-town life. The attempt to combine the best of rural and urban life sometimes resulted in the construction of self-contained, totally planned communities. Since residents usually commuted to city jobs, these developments were totally dependent upon trolleys, commuter trains, and increasingly the automobile. Ironically, design of such communities made every effort to deny the invention to which they owed their very existence.

Studies were undertaken showing how these ". . . areas could be planned so they would be insulated from the noise, fumes, and hazards of floods of automobiles." Radburn, New Jersey, the pioneering "city for the motor age," developed in 1929, was an early and ambitious planned community. Its design featured ". . . superblocks of 30–50 acres in which there were interior parks, where children could play without fear of falling under the wheels of the mechanical juggernaut."

Designed by Radburn's chief architect Clarence Stein, the city's gas station reflected the desire to avoid conflict with its residential environment. In fact, its sloping shingled roofs and stone walls complemented the community. Given a prominent corner in the complex, with its pumps hidden from view, it bears a remarkable similarity to a station design suggested for adoption in a *House and Garden* of 1925.

The gasoline station has been incorporated into a great many planned communities of significance, such as Rancho Santa Fe, New Mexico, and during the 1960s, Columbia, Maryland, and Reston, Virginia. Such stations have always reflected their communities' suburban, vernacular architecture.

The growth of suburbia fostered numerous small-scale shopping villages, reflecting both the scale and architecture of their suburban surroundings. These shopping centers at-

Fig. 58
Kansas City,
Missouri

Fig. 59
Westerville,
Ohio

tained their "quaint" quality by dealing with the shopper as a pedestrian, not a motorist. The gas station, providing an essential service to the suburbanite, was commonly part of these villages. Designed to function both at the pedestrian and vehicular scales, the gas station became a key transitional element of such centers.

A successful example of these self-contained off-street complexes was Dallas's 1931 Highland Park Village. Its gas station, a two-story white stucco structure capped by a red tile roof, reflected the Spanish theme of the village, while relating in scale to both pedestrian and motorist. The façades facing the pedestrian section of the Highland Park center contained a projecting balcony above a row of small windows that bore decorative wrought-iron grillwork. The building's street side featured massive arched drive-through openings.

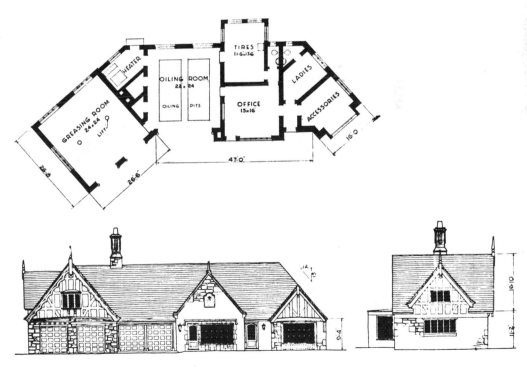

Figs. 60 & 61 Scarsdale, New York

Fig. 62 Westchester County, New York

ARCHITECTURE COMPETITION

NUMBER XI

Fig. 63
1928 design
competition
prize winner

The Highland Park station complemented the shopping complex while blending in with its residential surroundings.

Relating both to civic awareness and suburbanization was the concept of the planned, yet picturesque, "natural" country road: the parkway. This phenemenon appeared in the twenties, enabling the urban and suburban driver to enjoy an outing in the country. These carefully designed, meandering, tree-lined parkways paralleled the early City Beautiful park systems. Reflecting the same aesthetic concern, these scenic drives presented an alternative to the roads along which billboards and all sorts of incongruous structures were permitted.

After many motorists had their pastoral meanderings cut short when they ran out of gas, filling stations were built along the parkways. The Westchester County (New York) Park Commission, responsible for one of the most advanced and extensive parkway systems of its time, developed in the mid-1920s stations that won wide architectural acclaim. Per-

Fig. 64   Oberlin, Ohio

haps the most significant of these, designed by Penrose Stout, was constructed on the Hutchinson River Parkway. Sited at a wide point on the median, the station served traffic going in either direction. Built of local stone, this one-story structure features a gabled wood-shingled roof, small, shuttered windows, and a projecting bay window calling to mind a rambling country house. In an effort to preserve an unspoiled, natural appearance, the architect hid the pumps with latticed housing reminiscent of water wells and modeled the compressed air machine's casing on an old-fashioned water pump.

Many suburban developments were neither exclusive, elaborate retreats nor planned utopian projects like Radburn. Instead, most were neighborhoods that featured homes built in a wide variety of architectural styles. Domestic stations were especially appropriate in this kind of setting.

In 1928, the journal *Architecture* sponsored a competition for the design of a suburban station. One of the winning designs, adapting a typical New England saltbox, captured the nostalgic flavor of the simple rural life. A small sign on the front lawn bearing the name of the oil company provided the only clue to the building's function. The area behind the "house" was reserved for servicing automobiles. Even there, a traditional lean-to addition formed the canopy protecting the service drive.

During the thirties, many companies designed stations that echoed contemporary tastes in suburban homes. Because they presented a pleasant contrast to many of the garish designs of the time, these stations often won the praise of garden clubs and chambers of commerce. A clapboard station in Oberlin, Ohio, with its elegant porch and settee, could barely be distinguished from its neighboring residences. Although the proposed location of a gas station on the site originally sparked opposition, the station, when opened, was hailed as being "a credit to its neighborhood."

As early as 1925, Texaco developed a standard prototype, featuring colonial elements, which would blend into a domestic environment. Within two years, this model had an adobe or pueblo counterpart for use in the residential developments

Fig. 65   Chapel Hill, North Carolina

Long-distance travelers refueling at Texaco station, 1929. Courtesy Texaco, Inc.

A road map advertisement, National Petroleum News *(1932). Author's collection.*

A welcome rest stop during bad weather. Courtesy Richard J. S. Gutman.

ABOVE: *San Antonio "tree" station. Photo by author, 1978. Author's collection.*

LEFT: *Shell Oil's symbol, converted into a facade for a small 1930s station, Winston-Salem, North Carolina. Courtesy Eric N. DeLony, photographer, 1977.*

ABOVE LEFT: *A standardized "pagoda" station, popular during the 1920s, West Allis, Wisconsin. Courtesy Richard J. S. Gutman, photographer, 1977.*

BELOW LEFT: *"Mammy" station near Natchez, Mississippi. Courtesy Chester H. Liebs, photographer, 1977.*

BELOW: *"Last Gas Before Freeway" station, Houston. Stephen Edward Moskowitz, photographer, 1978. Author's collection.*

RIGHT: *1923 domed station, Dorchester, Massachusetts. Courtesy Richard J. S. Gutman, photographer, 1976.*

A flamboyant Art Deco Fina station, Shamrock, Texas. Courtesy Peter C. Papademetriou, photographer, 1977.

"Good Luck" gas station, Dallas. Photo by author, 1978. Author's collection.

ABOVE: *Nationally standardized Domestic-style station, Owego, New York. Photo by author, 1976. Author's collection.*

BELOW: *"Cottage" station, now a repair shop, Houston. Stephen Edward Moskowitz, photographer, 1978. Author's collection.*

Self-service Art Deco station, Houston. Photo by author, 1977. Author's collection.

ABOVE: *Walter Dorwin Teague's station design, now synonymous with Texaco. Stephen Edward Moskowitz, photographer, 1978. Author's collection.*

RIGHT: *Houston station, reflecting debt to Wright's projects. Stephen Edward Moskowitz, photographer, 1978. Author's collection.*

Night view of a Mobil station designed by Eliot Noyes, 1964.

Streetside clapboard station, Brookline, Massachusetts. Courtesy Richard J. S. Gutman, photographer, 1977.

ABOVE: *A Houston board-and-batten station, descendant of the early "cottage" stations. Stephen Edward Moskowitz, photographer, 1978. Author's collection.*

RIGHT: *Gas station recycled into auto service-and-supply store, Germantown, Pennsylvania. Photo by author, 1976. Author's collection.*

Houston Conoco station converted into a restaurant/disco. Photo by author, 1976. Author's collection.

Fig. 66   Manitow, Colorado

of the Southwest. Simple stucco walls with arched openings and protruding imitation roof poles linked the building to both the simple Indian residences of previous centuries and their successors, vernacular suburban homes.

At about the same time these Domestic stations were in vogue, a more direct design approach emerged: the "Functional" station. By the late 1930s and 1940s, the International Style had eclipsed all other styles. Champions of modernism argued in favor of more functional approaches to design and against the use of ornamentation and nostalgic, historical styles. By the early fifties, however, this movement had lost some of its momentum, and attempts to capture the best of Domestic and "Functional" stations were undertaken. Not merely "dressed" as domestic buildings, these stations are influenced by the "search for form" that characterized the movement away from the International Style.

A widely implemented Exxon prototype of the fifties displays the smooth, unadorned regularity of the functional aesthetic. Its office, though, has been distinguished from the service area by a flaring roof line that is repeated in the service canopy. The vocabulary of this design recalls the domestic work of Marcel Breuer in his attempts to humanize the austere International Style.

An often-used Shell design of this era employs a slightly more outspoken domestic imagery. Dramatically sloping shed roofs with overhanging eaves dominate the building. With its large, canted plate-glass windows, the roof form suggests the cathedral ceilings that adorned many contemporary suburban dream homes. A stylized red porcelain element bearing Shell's logo appears to be an abstraction of a chimney— a prominent element in the earlier Domestic stations. Rich with the iconographic value of hearth and home, this "chimney" adds visual interest, separating the office from the service bays. These two stations demonstrate the impact of the modern movement in architecture on Domestic station design.

The experimental prototypes developed for Texaco by designers Peter Muller-Munk Associates illustrate the same

Fig. 67   Detroit, Michigan

Fig. 68   1964 "Mattawan" station

phenomenon. They began opening in 1964. The stations contain a combination of elements—the "Functional" modern curtain wall, the Domestic, traditional, fieldstone masonry wall, and the mansard roof. Separate mansard-roofed canopies shelter the service drives.

During the mid-sixties Domestic styles experienced a resurgence of popularity. As in the past, a civic-awareness program played an important part in the style's rejuvenation. Lady Bird Johnson took a special interest in gas station design as part of a crusade to "beautify America." After the passage of the Highway Beautification Act of 1966, Mrs. Johnson invited oil-company executives to the White House to discuss the potential contribution that the nation's 210,000 gas stations could make toward the improvement of the country's landscape. Mrs. Johnson's consciousness-raising program, and a change in consumer tastes, led to a renewed interest in the design of Domestic stations.

A Texaco station in Houston exhibits the conflicts that result from the overlapping of styles. A bright-green shingled mansard roof crowns all the station's walls that are visible to traffic. This domesticating "hat" features dormer windows, which tend to reinforce the residential imagery. Examination of the building from a usually unexposed side reveals that the superstructure is merely an appliqué, tacked on to an austere building. Many "Functional" stations were brought up to date by adding a few appropriate symbols of domesticity, such as a shingled roof, a fieldstone façade, or lanterns. Often shrubbery was added to the finished product, softening the "Functional" imagery.

By the late sixties, large petroleum companies had developed standard procedures for converting "Functional" boxes into sprawling ranch houses. When completed, many of these converted stations appeared almost identical to their newly constructed counterparts. Shell's "suburban house" service station displays a pair of gently sloping gable roofs, one over the office, with the other higher roof over the service bays, reminiscent of a split-level ranch house. A large "chimney" serves to separate the office from the service area. Instead of

Figs. 69 & 70 Before and after, Houston, Texas

Fig. 71
Houston, Texas

the red porcelain abstraction of the fifties' model, white brick forms the chimney. The domestic imagery is obvious, yet well integrated with the requirements for a modern station. Areas of planting around the station grounds serve to reinforce the residential aspects of the design.

Gulf's board-and-batten model perhaps best illustrates the evolution of the early cottage to the modern station. A box sided with large, aluminum, earth-toned board-and-batten panels forms the building. Mansard roofs of asphalt tile printed with wooden patterns adorn the structure and canopies. The board-and-batten is often considered to be a

hallmark of the Picturesque movement in America; the rough-hewn wood shingle is an element associated with rustic building. The contemporary Gulf stations project, by use of similar materials, an image of the Picturesque rustic cottage. Technological innovations as well as the expansion of the station's program have, however, totally changed the methods of achieving a residential effect. A metal sheathing, not wood, actually creates the earth-toned board-and-batten siding. Similarly, asphalt imprinted with a wooden grain imitates rustic, hand-split shingles. Originally, stations of a smaller residential scale contained these Domestic elements. The present Domestic station, by contrast, has become a caricature of a house by adding exaggerated, overscaled, overtly residential elements to a basically industrial building.

Throughout its history, the Domestic station's popularity has stemmed from its almost universal acceptability. Because they are deemed neither tasteless nor intimidating, Domestic stations have seemed the perfect neighborhood service station. Though the appeal of their theme has been constant, the manner in which these stations have conveyed their residential imagery has changed with the times. Many of them were clothed in quaint, Picturesque garb; others took on the various styles of their suburban surroundings. Today, Domestic stations rely to a great extent upon residential symbols and imagery tacked on to distinctly nonresidential buildings.

Though contemporary Domestic stations seem a distinctive, readily identifiable type, they owe a debt to the modern or "Functional" movement in architecture. The influence of functionalism brought the stations' technical apparatus—once embarrassments to be hidden away behind water wells and latticed sheds—out in the open and incorporated them into designs that were at once attractive, unified, and practical. Of course, functionalism's impact upon the design of Domestic stations is only a small part of another aspect of gas station design. The celebration of the station's industrial form has had an interesting and complex history in its own right.

Fig. 72   Houston, Texas

5 The "Functional"

For many years, motorists bought gas from airplanes, windmills, Greek temples, civic monuments, and rustic cottages. "Functional" stations ushered in a new look: They celebrated the technology that complemented the machine they served. During the 1930s, *Architectural Forum* proclaimed, "In recent years, a new type of station has made its appearance. It is clean, unassuming, and has the inestimable virtue of looking like a filling station."

"Functional" designs were smooth, clean, and, like a machine, pared of superfluous parts. What's more, this approach allowed a wide variety of styles: the simple, unadorned brick or prefabricated metal and glass box; the severe yet elegant International Style; the freer designs of Frank Lloyd Wright and others; the abstractly ornamented Moderne. In reality the "Functional" station was no more a functional machine-age building than the Domestic station was a home or the Respectable station a civic monument.

Two basic types of buildings—the brick and stucco box and the steel-framed glass box—characterized the earliest "Functional" stations. The virtue of these structures stemmed from their practicality and economy rather than their appearance. A 1926 *Architectural Forum* commented, "Good taste as well as cost of building would seem to indicate that a simple, straightforward style of architecture should be followed in the design of a filling and service station." In a prefabricated station, the aesthetic reflected the speed with which it had been erected. Leaving cables, tie rods, corrugated metal roofs, and wall panels fully exposed, these stations became celebrations of the technology that created them.

Carefully groomed shrubbery and manicured flower beds often surrounded such stations. An apology rather than a contradiction, this overlay softened the impact of the structure's frankly industrial appearance. Sometimes this dual imagery carried over to the building itself, when trim on the service drive canopy created the appearance of a garden trellis.

As the station building expanded to offer a full range of automotive services, the materials and technology of the

Fig. 73 Pittsburgh, Pennsylvania

Fig. 74   San Francisco, California

Union Metal Design No. R-236.   One of a dozen pleasing designs.

These Stations Close Leases

WHEN you run onto one of those tough situations where the owner or neighborhood objects to a gasoline station, show him a Union Metal Ornamental Filling Station. The pleasing design will go a long way toward closing that lease. And the same pleasing design brings business to you, day after day, night after night. Moreover, these *ornamental* filling stations carry no price penalty. The cost of a Union Metal Filling Station, *erected,* is no greater than many less pleasing stations. For these buildings come to you complete—not an extra to buy; a real saving in time and money. Let us tell you *all* about Union Metal Ornamental Filling Stations.

Send for Catalog No. 55. It tells all about Union Metal Ornamental Filling Stations.

There is a limited amount of open territory available to agents for Union Metal Ornamental Filling Stations. If you are interested in a rapidly growing business, write for our best proposition for agents.

THE UNION METAL MANUFACTURING CO.
General Offices and Factory, Canton, Ohio
Chicago Office — 230 South Clark Street

UNION METAL
ORNAMENTAL FILLING STATIONS

November 17, 1926   13

Fig. 75   1926 ad for prefabricated station

Fig. 76   1932 ad for auto servitorium

small, prefab station found application in the larger building. Steel, glass, and porcelain were combined to erect these modern stations. These unadorned, rectangular, steel frame boxes with flat roofs housed service bays and the station office behind porcelain-trimmed glass walls. As with their earlier, smaller counterparts, steel formed the clearly expressed framework whereas glass and porcelain infill panels formed the walls. Often smooth, easily maintained porcelain panels provided an element of color around the bases and rooflines, where the use of glass was impractical. This popular, versatile material provided a new cladding for modernizing and expanding conventionally constructed brick and stucco stations. Openly revealing the station's operation, the building was turned into a continuous advertisement for itself.

The manufacturers of these stations pointed to their practicality, claiming "inefficient, traditional ideas have been discarded, every detail of the new super-service station has been developed to serve its special purpose." This honesty of expression formed the basis of an emerging "Functional" building style.

The subsequent Modern movement of the thirties, combining functionalism with a machine-inspired aesthetic, became known as the International Style. The Museum of Modern Art (MOMA) in New York officially introduced this European concept of modernism to America with its 1932 show, "Modern Architecture: International Exhibition." Henry-Russell Hitchcock and Philip Johnson, then director of the Department of Architecture and Design for the museum, authored a book titled *The International Style: Architecture Since 1922*, which defined this revolutionary style. International Style proponents argued that architecture should emphasize light, elegant spaces rather than mass or solidity, that regularity and repetition should be favored over symmetry, and that a structure's intrinsic elegance should derive from the materials themselves rather than applied ornamentation. It took the frank industrialism that was so much a part of the early "Functional" stations and converted it into a sophisticated style. The museum exhibit, which traveled

Fig. 77 Cleveland, Ohio

across the nation, and the Hitchcock-Johnson book were pivotal in introducing these concepts of modernism to the mainstream of American architecture.

The MOMA show of 1932 included a Standard Oil station that was superficially indistinguishable from many earlier prefab models. Designed as a prototype by the American firm of Clauss and Daub in 1931, this station had a continuous glass wall that created a light, elegant volume. Colored enamel plates formed a narrow red cornice under which a white band announced the company name in red lettering. In contrast to the prefabs of the twenties, in which the structural steel skeleton framed the glass, here the elegant curtain wall skin stands free of the building's concrete support system. This Standard Oil station embodies the principles of the International Style and illustrates the evolution of the bold functionalism of the 1920s into an academic doctrine.

Although the exhibit was a major influence on American architecture, few examples of pure International Style buildings emerged in the United States. Rather than adopt the style, many prominent American architects adapted it, using it as a point of departure, creating a "modern" yet less revolutionary, more humane style. Other influences on postwar architects included a strong interest in Frank Lloyd Wright's renewed creative activity, espousing the use of natural materials. In addition, an interest in traditional vernacular building was spurred by the "discovery" of the little-known architectural traditions of California.

Eldridge Spencer, a respected California architect, took the International Style as his point of departure for a Yosemite National Park station built around 1941. This station features much glass, without conveying machine imagery; its natural, unassuming image is unmistakably modern. Instead of the smooth enamel panels and steel mullions of the Standard Oil station exhibited at MOMA, Spencer's station displays a trim of warm Douglas fir and redwood. The forms of this flat-roofed, transparent building are clearly that of the International Style, but the selection of materials with natural finishes creates a more relaxed composition.

Fig. 78 Combination gas station—restaurant rendering

"No one's driving enjoyment is increased by the haphazard strings of diners, gasoline stations . . . and billboards which have been permitted on both sides of our highways," wrote architect William Lescaze in 1942. Lescaze, whose work had appeared in the original International Style show, was among the most innovative practitioners of the style. In keeping with his position as an advocate of improved roadside buildings, in 1943 he designed an elegant combination gas station–restaurant. The concise renderings of his proposed station show planes of International Style glass walls intersecting more natural stone ones. The aesthetic of the International Style combined with a softer look to create a station that was admired for its "use of fine, textured materials," which, the commentary continued, "makes this a pleasant place to drive in to."

A project of the mid-forties by the New York firm of Ely Jacques Kahn and Robert Allan Jacobs for Pittsburgh Plate Glass, also combined eating with refueling. The building, with its large expanses of glass recalling the International Style and early prefab stations, provides plenty of light while showing the hydraulic equipment at work from the outside. In other ways, though, the architects took definite steps away from a rigid glass and steel vocabulary. A prominently placed, structural red-glass wall with a map painted gold stands inside the station. A large canopy conveying "the powerful motif of the airplane wing" provides an even more dramatic departure from the International Style. The aerodynamic form of the prominent canopy has made the imagery of the machine age more explicit.

Born in Vienna, Richard Neutra worked with avant-garde European architects before coming to work briefly with Frank Lloyd Wright in the early 1920s. An architect with a profound understanding of the International Style, Neutra evidences in his work his development of the mode into a highly personalized idiom. One of his gas station designs constructed in Bakersfield, California, combines a frank expression of materials and academic clarity with a sense of drama. A large, dramatic, corrugated-metal canopy, recalling many of his houses' balconies, acts as much as a billboard as a sheltering device, because of its height. This handsome station blends the tenets of the International Style with the distinctive vision of a great designer.

R. Buckminster Fuller, famous for his geodesic dome and designs of machines for living, championed a design philosophy that, like the International Style, addressed modernism and the expression of technology. This philosophy dealt not with the refined, abstract elements of industrial technology but with the nuts and bolts of the machine, stressing literal rather than metaphoric aspects of modern technology. The jagged, exposed masts and cables that characterize this mode seem, at first, the antithesis of the smooth veneers of the International Style. Though these two styles certainly use different approaches, their underlying purpose —the architectural celebration of the machine—links them at least from a theoretical standpoint.

Figs. 79 & 80 Chicago, Illinois

Chicago architect Bertrand Goldberg's 1938 prototype for Standard Oil presents a striking example of a similar design philosophy. The clearly expressed structure consists of two steel masts, from which hang cables supporting the building. This structural system eliminated the need for a full foundation. The virtually portable structure makes great visual impact, with only a minimal commitment to its site. The station's tall masts, projecting far into the air, bear neon lights proclaiming its function: G-A-S. A generous use of glass reveals the mysteries of its inner workings to customers and passing motorists. Goldberg's design exploited functionalism as an attention-attracting device.

A combination of romanticism and machine-age precision characterizes Viennese-born Rudolph Schindler's essays on service station design. Schindler, like Neutra, was trained in Europe; upon coming to this country, he spent five years in Frank Lloyd Wright's studio. Among his several station designs, the 1933 Union Oil project illustrates an intricate solution while clearly showing the Wrightian—De Stijl influence. In this design, huge, soaring canopies project from

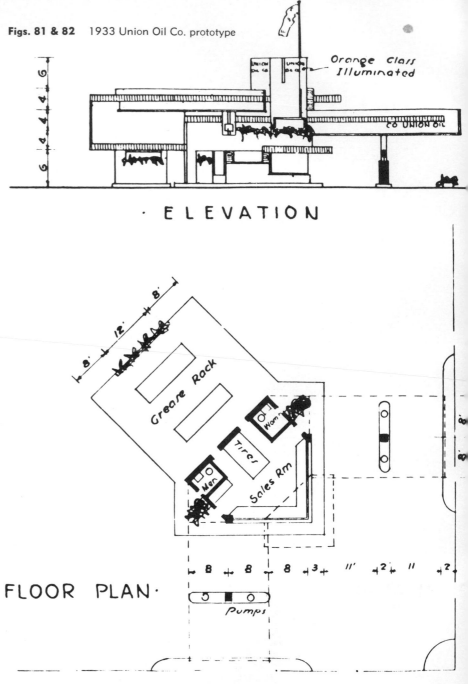

Figs. 81 & 82 1933 Union Oil Co. prototype

· E L E V A T I O N

FLOOR PLAN·

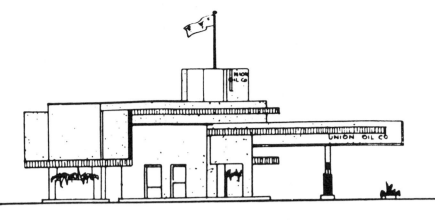

· E L E V A T I O N ·

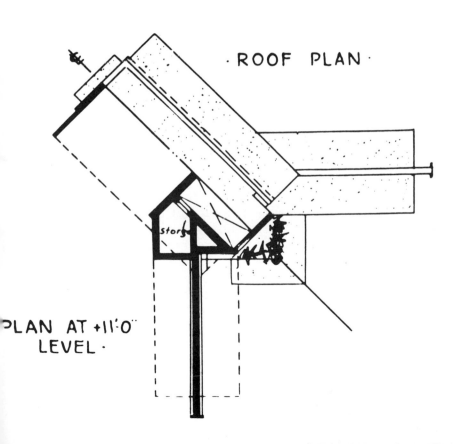

· ROOF PLAN ·

Stor.

PLAN AT +11'·0"
LEVEL ·

a large, central glass tower that emits a hearthlike orange glow. (Incidentally, orange was a Union Oil color.) The tall central tower and horizontal canopies of the station suggest an obvious parallel to many of Wright's earlier Prairie houses, where the horizontal elements appeared to soar out from their central anchoring chimney. Plants hanging from and accentuating the station's complicated, intersecting roof planes give this project an added dimension while relating it to Schindler's somewhat more tentative, earlier but similar project for "a gasoline station constructed of steel, glass and plants."

To Frank Lloyd Wright, the gas station was to play an important role in forming the restructured, less urban American society that he envisioned. "The roadside service station," he declared in his autobiography, first published in 1943, "may be in embryo the future city service distribution center. Each station may grow into a well-designed, convenient neighborhood distribution center naturally developing as meeting place, restaurant, restroom. . . ." The flamboyance of Wright's projects for gas stations reflects the civic importance he attached to the building type. Wright began his first station projects in 1928 (a compact urban building and a more complete rural one) and eventually incorporated the design as part of his utopian Broadacre City. Wright's early design features exposed trusses supporting cantilevered canopies that extend from the office. Large "masts" bearing neon-tube sails articulate the cantilever's main support and serve to attract attention to the station. In order to keep a continuous, flexible, flowing space, the gas was to be supplied not from conventional pumps but from flexible overhead hoses suspended from the cantilevered canopies. Could it be that the famous architect saw petroleum—which he lyrically described as "the wealth of states, the health of nations"—as the machine-age counterpart to the cow's milk? Flowing from hanging hoses, the petroleum came to the motorist as the milk came to the farm boy. As Wright asked, "How many trusties and lusties besides her lawful calf have pulled away at her teats these thousands of years? . . ."

Twenty-eight years later, Frank Lloyd Wright designed a filling station for a Cloquet, Minnesota, retailer. It was a modified working model that could become a standard prefab station. The three-level steel and cement block structure featuring a glass-walled observation lounge anchored a soaring thirty-two-feet copper canopy. Fire codes prevented the planned overhead gasoline hoses from being realized. A highly stylized illuminated pylon, reminiscent of the neon sails bearing the Phillips 66 name, reached sixty feet into the air.

Although the "cool" modernism of the International Style never dominated American architecture, it had a profound influence. By substituting indigenous materials for flashy ones, or by combining glass and steel with stone and wood, or by using highly individual dramatic elements (such as soaring canopies) to highlight more conventional buildings, architects brought animation and personality to the "Functional" gas station while still creating modern designs. A sense of drama and movement away from the clean func-

tionalism of the International Style, combined with the exaggerated illustration of structure typical of the technological expressionists, became a dominant theme that culminated in the search for form of the 1950s. In many ways, Frank Lloyd Wright—who, with his highly personal forms, had been seeking to break the confines of the "box" as evidenced by his station designs—was the precursor of this movement. Wright had for some time been using dramatically soaring roof forms corresponding to the modulation of interior spaces.

The search for drama and animation, combined with "cooler" modern influences, led to the development of the fifties' archetypal roadside building. A shed roof, with its high point on the roadside, rapidly sloping downward toward the rear of the building, dominates this relatively simple edifice. This Wrightian modulation of space creates a directly functional structure. Largest where it needs to be most dramatic and attract attention, the space becomes increasingly enclosed, housing the service function in the rear. Canted windows, reducing glare, and paired columns, dramatizing the structure, add to the building's visual interest. These structures, epitomized by Carvel or the McDonald's of the fifties, became at once the roadside sign *and* the building. Although such looks are often considered the iconography of fast food, service stations applied the same principles, sometimes changing the plan to accommodate the station's functions.

Phillips Petroleum Company applied these principles in a widely implemented scheme. A dramatically soaring V-shaped canopy dominates these stations. The canopy appears to be cantilevered from trusslike supports that rise from the pump islands. Actually triangular truss assemblies that seem to penetrate through the canopy's outermost point support the canopy while dramatically displaying the Phillips logo. In this scheme, the arrangement of the office and service bays varies depending on the site. The large, often canted, plate-glass windows and the arrangement of service bays around the office indicate a debt to Wright's "search for form."

Art Deco, or Moderne, paralleled the International Style and the technological expressionism of the Modern movement (1920s to 1940s). Although it also symbolically celebrated the machine, its principles were quite different. Its major impetus came from the 1925 Exposition Internationale des Arts Décoratifs et Industriels Modernes in Paris. Unmistakably modern in its opposition to traditional architecture, Art Deco reinterpreted previous design styles rather than rejecting them. Reflecting the machine age with its smooth surfaces, Art Deco did not directly reveal or celebrate a building's structure; instead, it sheathed the edifice with a machine-finished covering. The Moderne had two distinct aspects: Zig-zag and Streamlined.

Zig-zag Moderne, which appeared primarily during the twenties and thirties, represented a direct and violent opposition to International Style principles. An adaptation of traditional conservative styles, Zig-zag Moderne was a contemporary idiom for the 1930s office building, just as the 1950s adaptation of the International Style became the formula for modern corporate architecture. Although the gas stations designed by this method were exciting, lyrical, and sometimes kinky extravaganzas, like the architect-designed prototypes related to the International Style, they were rarely standardized on a broad basis. Typically, these stations dis-

Figs. 84 & 85
Houston, Texas

Fig. 86 Houston, Texas

played mechanically repetitive applied ornamentation noted for its crisp angularity. On occasion, the harsh façade received further relief by the use of elliptical windows. In the more vibrant stations, neon tubing formed the ornamentation. Consistent with this trim, the building formed a blocky geometric mass. The structure was in no way expressed but rather clad, with a variety of opaque materials. Porcelain—in a range of rich colors including cream, blue, yellow, or chartreuse—smooth, buff-colored stucco, terra-cotta, or glazed tiles were among the façade coverings.

By far the most attractive and plentiful of the Moderne stations are the Streamlined models of the 1930s and 1940s. Standardized company stations introduced the Sreamlined Moderne to many communities. Streamlined designs discard the ornamentation of the Zig-zag in favor of smooth, sweeping curved forms that create cohesive packages. These buildings do not celebrate or reveal the technology of their structural systems; a continuous slick sheathing unifies all the parts of the building. As their name implies, these Streamlined stations project a sensation of speed through their aerodynamic imagery, conveying an aura of futuristic transportation. Perhaps for this reason, followers of the International Style found the Streamlined more palatable than other Art Deco variations. Though Streamlined stations often retained the blocky massing of the earlier Zig-zag, their slick, swooping surfaces created the image of machined packages.

A typical Streamlined design implemented by the Gulf Oil Company features smoothly rounded corners and large expanses of glass terminating in half-circles. The display windows curve around the station's corners, uniting the front and sides. Bands of stripes, one of the Streamlined style's trademarks, follow the curved contours of the building. A tall, blocky tower reminiscent of the Zig-zag defines the station's entrance. The tower, composed of glass block, combines with the other expanses of glass to create an impressive edifice.

During the 1930s a group of designers emerged who took the Streamlined Moderne as a basis for creating smoothly

Fig. 87 Brighton, Michigan

Fig. 88   Pittsburgh, Pennsylvania

packaged commercial buildings. Much like the members of the European Bauhaus school, these industrial designers envisioned a marriage of art, architecture, and industry that would bring a scientific efficiency to everyday items. Their work was by no means confined to buildings but involved the efficient packaging of appliances and machines ranging from can openers to airplanes, ships, and cars.

The application of streamlining principles to the automobile resulted in the bringing together of discrete elements such as fenders, doors, and straight windshields into an efficient, cohesive whole. Perhaps the best known of such commercially produced autos was the 1934 Chrysler Airflow, designed by Carl Breer and Norman Bel Geddes. Although this change in auto design did not at first meet with public acceptance (the Airflow was not a financial success), by 1937 most mass-produced cars looked streamlined.

It follows that the industrial designer would apply his scientific concepts of packaging to the gasoline station. In 1934, Norman Bel Geddes undertook a thorough study of the service station for the Socony Vacuum Oil Company, today known as Mobil. Using the analytical approach typical of the industrial designer, Geddes summarized the pertinent facts about station design in twenty-four charts that dealt with image and visibility, lighting, construction, and traffic circulation. Controlled by strategic plantings and different road surfaces, traffic flow relates both to the street and internal circulation. Quick refueling operations stand apart from the more complex service functions; the services and accessories available at the station are clearly visible from the fuel pumps.

A subsequent design for use near the 1939 New York World's Fair (itself an industrial designer's Streamlined extravaganza) incorporates Socony-Mobil's symbol, the drum. The station comprised three ovoid, or tearlike, buildings arranged at the corners of a triangular site. The drum, which accentuates the main building, is subsumed by the tearlike form, which was thought to achieve aerodynamic perfection and became an acceptable form of the streamlined.

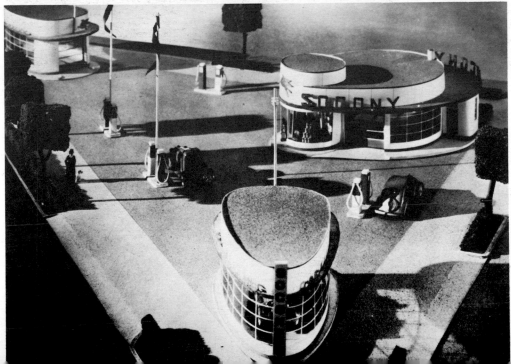

Fig. 89   Flushing Meadows, New York

Mobilgas
SOCONY-VACUUM

Mobilubrication   Mobiloil   Mobilgas

Safe
tire
repair
BONES

Fig. 91   1934 design for an urban "Servicenter"

69

Filling stations have usually been built on corner lots because of the large driveway area that they require. In larger cities, such sites are scarce and much more expensive than interior lots. In 1934 Esso commissioned Raymond Loewy to design a prototype suited to a cramped Manhattan site. In response to this design problem, Loewy's compact "servicenter" featured a central rotating turntable with a three-car capacity. During one rotation an automobile received gas, oil, and water returning completely serviced to the street within two minutes. More extensive service provided at the rear of the structure is reached via the turntable. The service center was housed in an elegant, Streamlined building. To compensate for the lost advertising value of the traditional corner location, a gently curving white porcelain tower, featuring Esso in blue letters and a full-length red arrow pointing to the rotary entrance, dominated the building's façade. An approaching driver would be drawn in by a curved, horizontally lined wall emphasizing the intriguing rotary beyond. The two stations built in New York City testify to the aptness of industrial designer Loewy's problem-solving method.

A prototype Texaco model designed by Walter Dorwin Teague has achieved the status of America's most familiar service station. It features a smooth, white exterior with elegant trim. A streamlined crown—composed of three plain green bands encircling the building, red stars evenly placed above the bands, and bold red lettering all set off against a white background—establishes corporate identity. Teague's stations could be adapted to every part of the country and were composed of a variety of materials depending on site and building conditions. Truly sophisticated industrial packages, these stations could be made of any material so long as they retained their smooth, white veneer. Porcelain enamel, stucco, or painted brick were all suitable. When climate required, a canopy could be added that extended forward from the building's cornice, carrying the distinctive three green bands around its smooth corners. Teague designed prototypes of this basic description for every conceivable site: two models for corner lots, two for mid-block, and one for high-

Despite scientific practicality, neither of the schemes Norman Bel Geddes created for Mobil was realized. Some of the findings, however, must have been useful to New York architect Frederick Frost, who developed a more conservative but visually exciting prototype for Mobil. Again featuring the drum motif, this model incorporates all the gas station functions in one structure. Contained within the mass of the building, the drum forms a dramatically curving façade that calls attention to the building while conveying the corporate identity.

Fig. 90   New York, New York

Fig. 92 1950s Gulf model

Fig. 93 Tampa, Florida

way locations. *Architectural Forum* presented the designs in 1937 and stated that Teague had developed a series of stations "which could be build in any part of the United States, in any location, of any material, on any shaped plot, with any number of service bays or none—and still maintain its identity as a typical Texaco station." Teague's Texaco station represents perhaps the most handsome and popular example of the industrial designer's art. They are simple, practical, and have an unmistakable modern look. The greatest tribute to Teaguc's Texaco station, though, is that to millions of motorists it became an immediately recognizable symbol of Texaco products.

Fig. 94 Palo Alto, California

72

The 1950s saw the coexistence of this modified Stream-lined box with the more flamboyant designs related to the International Style and Frank Lloyd Wright. By the end of the decade, however, the stylistic antecedents of most stations had become more generalized, less traceable to a particular design theory. Representative models of this era suggest a merger of the two fundamental "Functional" styles, each having roots as far back as the twenties: the transparent International Style–related structure and its more massive counterpart, the solid, Moderne (or Art Deco) building. In a sense, a "new classicism" reconciled the two trends.

In the late 1950s Welton Becket and Associates designed a gas station in Palo Alto, California, that combines glass boxes and solid boxes. A straightforward rectangular structure contains the main building, housing office, salesroom, working areas, and restrooms. Black tubular steel columns form the station's structural frame, with plate glass filling in most of the sections and red glazed brick accenting the rest of the building. White porcelain trim caps the building. The combination of clear glass panels deriving from the prefab box and the solid walls reminiscent of the more conventional box suggests the tendency to bring together these two divergent design approaches.

In 1964 Eliot Noyes created a widely implemented design for Mobil that affected some 19,000 stations throughout the world. Like Teague's design for Texaco, Noyes's prototype was adaptable to every conceivable type of setting. The plans for this station were flexible enough to be used for either the remodeling of an existing station or the construction of new ones.

Though the layout of these stations varied widely, their basic features remained constant. In all of them a series of separate glass panels reveals office, service, and refreshment areas. Alternating solid panels of wood, stone, brick, or any other viable material provide a contrast to the smooth expanses of glass. A series of station accessories combines with the powerfully detailed building to create a corporate identity through the repetition of Mobil's longtime symbol, the oil

Fig. 97 Cynwood, Pennsylvania

drum. Recalling the drum motif, huge circular canopies over the refueling areas serve double duty as lighting fixtures. Aluminum and glass drums—which form the gas pumps, oil racks, and attendant's booths—all echo the corporate motif.

During the past fifteen years a series of architect-designed stations has been built using the building itself, rather than the repetition of corporate imagery, to attract the motorist. While they suggest a continuation of the post–International Style search for a more animated modern form, they also recall the naïve Fantastic stations. These modern "Functional" stations base their attraction not on whimsy but rather on a serious, self-conscious, "architectonic" appeal.

Vincent G. Kling and Associates designed for Atlantic Refining Company a prototype that opened in Philadelphia in 1964. Triangular in plan, the building has sliding glass panel doors throughout. The salesroom occupies the section facing the main thoroughfare and is visible to travelers going in either direction. To the rear of the office are service bays accessible from either side of the triangle. A huge, truncated pyramidal roof dominates the entire design. The building itself, not any of the accessories, acts as sign. The dramatic roof recalls Frank Lloyd Wright's earlier essays in roadside architecture and perhaps more directly his 1950s Cloquet gas station, which has roof planes similar to his other work of this decade. The building has its own dramatic advertising value.

Miës van der Rohe undertook several projects that addressed the problem of the drive-in building. In 1934, while still in Europe, Miës entered a gas station design in a competition; in 1945–46, after coming to this country, he produced a dramatic drive-in restaurant project for Indianapolis; in 1967–68, he executed a commission for an Esso station in Montreal, Quebec. A station-restaurant combination along the Tri-State Toll Road in Illinois, designed by architect David Haid, strongly resembles one of these Miësian designs. The long, smooth, glass and steel structure that dramatically spans the freeway, houses the restaurant and connects the two service stations at either end. As in Kling's Atlantic sta-

tion, the striking visual impressions that this building presents renders the use of large signs unnecessary.

An award-winning station of 1973, designed by Lawrence Booth of Booth & Nagle in collaboration with the Center for Advanced Research in Design, creates a strong impression by its direct expression of both structure and construction. This advanced, well-received Chicago station is made up of a kit of parts that can be assembled in several ways according to the requirements of station size and site. A dominant spaceframe roof structure consists of thirteen-foot triangular modules supported by columns. The supports combine with gas pumps and lighting fixtures as part of the column assembly. Although the pumps extend to the ground, the petroleum flows from overhead hoses, as Wright had envisioned for his

Fig. 98   Mount Prospect, Illinois

stations. The station's vivid expression of its structure recalls the early prefabricated stations as well as other "Functional" stations where the building's structural features dominated. Here, though, the framework is clearly overscaled and abstract; its purpose is not so much to support the building as to serve as a symbol of structure. The building creates a poetic celebration of its materials and method of construction.

The Architects Collaborative of Cambridge, Massachusetts, designed a series of stations for Merit Petroleum in the Boston area. The architectural elements of the stations seem tremendously exaggerated. Brutalistic buildings, made of ribbed concrete block and glass, house these stations' offices. Formed by large, inverted concrete channels, the imposing pump-island canopies are as much tastefully integrated "billboards" screaming for attention as they are a functioning part of each station's architecture. These canopies relate to highway iconography, resembling the dramatic elements that support freeway bridges and overpasses. Though the massive structure of the Merit stations is in contrast to the much lighter mode of the Booth design, both designs are related by their use of outspokenly modernistic forms to announce company affiliation and to draw attention to themselves.

"Functional" stations evolved from simple, apologetically groomed buildings to wild architectonic statements. In the intervening years, the station passed through a series of different phases, each reflective of a larger and more significant trend in contemporary architecture.

At one time or another, almost every prominent American architect or industrial designer has engaged in gas station design. Often the stations were the only local example of a particular design approach. "Functional" gas stations reflected trends ranging from the elegant International Style to a more rustic and natural postwar style influenced by the work of Wright and others associated with him. Parallel to these modes were the Moderne stations, especially those introduced by industrial designers. Although the designs were generally conservative, they had more of a dramatic impact on our landscape than any other type of building. These simply stated structures, lasting in popularity from the thirties through the fifties, gave way to the simple, seemingly rational buildings of the late 1950s and 1960s. Recently, modern architects using exaggerated architectural elements have designed stations that are more extreme versions of the "Functional" station.

Fig. 99   Cambridge, Massachusetts

6 Preservation

The American gasoline station, so much a part of our every-day lives, is at once highly sophisticated and disarmingly simple. The rediscovery of this building type is part of a renewed interest in the familiar. Although it may lack fine details, the gas station projects an image to the motorist. A series of themes emerges, each catching the motorist's attention in a distinctive manner.

The earliest image projected by the gas station was a Fantastic one, emphatically attracting attention in a naïve way. Stations were built in the shape of boats, lighthouses, airplanes, and space stations. Buildings taking the form of gas pumps, measuring and gas cans, tank cars, and three-dimensional representations of company trademarks, such as shell-shaped Shell stations and the dinosaur of Sinclair stations, glorified automobile transportation and the related burgeoning petroleum industry. Filling stations in the form of icebergs, southern mammys, teepees, and pagodas portrayed natural formations, cultural themes, and exotic architecture.

Creating an aura of prestige and making an imposing addition to the roadside, Respectable stations reflected social and marketing values. These elegant stations bestowed prestige upon their brand of gas. Receiving their impetus from the City Beautiful movement, these stations were part of the drive to make the structure a civic asset, a goal often achieved through the use of architectural features commonly found on buildings of great civic importance—banks, monuments, and city halls. Classical monuments and domed extravaganzas created elaborate stations: Spanish bell towers and elegant pedimented porticos lent grandeur.

A different breed of the Respectable station often borrowed the dignity of an adjacent building. The Romanesque forms of Stanford University's buildings and the Gothic buildings of Princeton University were restated in scaled down form in nearby gasoline stations; more recently a miniature Astrodome (Texaco) and a miniature Three Rivers Stadium (Gulf) provide gas to visiting sports fans.

Suggesting the values of hearth and home, the Domestic station minimized community opposition by blending in with neighboring residences while serving as a symbol of familiarity to the traveler in an unfamiliar area. These stations ranged from the rustic, irregular cottage with ties to the English Picturesque movement to standardized company models. More recently, Lady Bird Johnson's beautification program gave an impetus to ranch and split-level stations, which took on the animation of their suburban surroundings.

When first introduced, the "Functional" filling station was hailed as a building that had the inestimable virtue of looking like what it was. This design approach was championed by the modern movement in architecture. Frank Lloyd Wright, Richard Neutra, Bertrand Goldberg, William Lescaze, Kahn & Jacobs, and Rudolph Schindler were among the prominent architects involved in the design of modern, "Functional" stations. Another approach to modern design was the Moderne, featuring curves suggesting speed and an aesthetic of futurism, as executed by industrial designers. Norman Bel Geddes, Raymond Loewy, and Walter Dorwin Teague all produced Streamlined Moderne extravaganzas. The most widely implemented of these stations is the previously discussed Texaco model devised by Teague, its white sheathing giving a fitting backdrop to the green bands and red stars that have become synonymous with Texaco.

With time, the gasoline station has projected its image in many different ways. Individual "mom and pop" stations built toward the beginning of this century express the mood of the early automotive era, when the car was more a plaything for the brave and adventurous than a practical conveyance. Today's stations, the product of a changed society, are designed for superhighways by large corporations. Neighborhood gas stations, once considered all too common, are now becoming an endangered species. David Macauley's cartoon, which illustrates a simple "Functional" station as an overgrown ruin being nostalgically examined by tourists, reflects this attitude and recalls the romantic portrayal of eighteenth- and nineteenth-century picturesque ruins. With oil companies constantly updating their own image, even the more recent gas stations face an uncertain future and deserve preservationists' support.

American preservation in its early years concerned itself primarily with patriotic shrines and artifacts. It generally calls to mind the restoration of isolated monuments rich with associative value, such as the early rehabilitation of Independence Hall or the Mount Vernon Ladies Association's heroic efforts to save and enshrine George Washington's home. Today, such grand buildings are still of vital importance (in fact, the more time passes, the more valuable they become); however, the modern preservation movement concerns itself with a wider spectrum of structures.

Throughout history, the character of buildings has changed, reflecting the taste, technology, and culture of their times. As our life-styles changes, these physical reminders of bygone eras acquire added importance. Preservation, therefore, does not only apply to a few isolated monuments, but to an increasingly broad spectrum, including twentieth-century buildings, that constitutes our built environment. Our more recent heritage must be preserved for future generations.

Traditionally, however, preservationists have viewed the

Fig. 100
From **Great Moments in Architecture** by David Macauley

automobile and its habits as a threat to their own projects. How many architecturally rich small towns and urban centers have been left to decay as motorists drive to strip shopping centers and malls lining freeways on the outskirts of town? Nonetheless, a realistic preservationist must recognize that this century's commercial architecture reflects modern culture as much as older buildings typify yesteryear's. The gas station, itself the premier drive-in building, has a history and rich design heritage of its own; as a significant part of the built environment, it is worthy of preservation.

Preservation efforts range from the physical and historical documentation of a building to the actual restoration or adaptive reuse of original structures. The federal govern-

Fig. 101
Near a
New York State
highway

ment, with the founding of the Historic American Building Survey (HABS) in 1933, and the similar, subsequently created Historic American Engineering Record (HAER), initiated a preservation program to document "buildings and objects of national significance." The measured drawings and photographs produced by HABS eventually become part of a permanent archive housed in the Library of Congress. Originally this was a public works project for unemployed architects; today professors and college students conduct the program's fieldwork during the summer. Included among the select artifacts are several gas stations. In the near future, HABS may undertake an extensive project in gas station documentation. A team could travel along old routes, stopping not only to refuel but to add a cross-section of these significant buildings to our country's archives.

Recognition and landmark status on a local, state, or national level offer varying degrees of protection to many

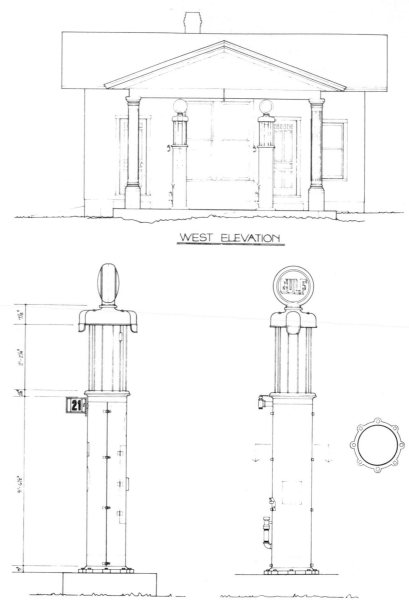

WEST ELEVATION

DETAILS OF GAS PUMP

Figs. 102 & 103   Drawings for station in Augusta County, Virginia

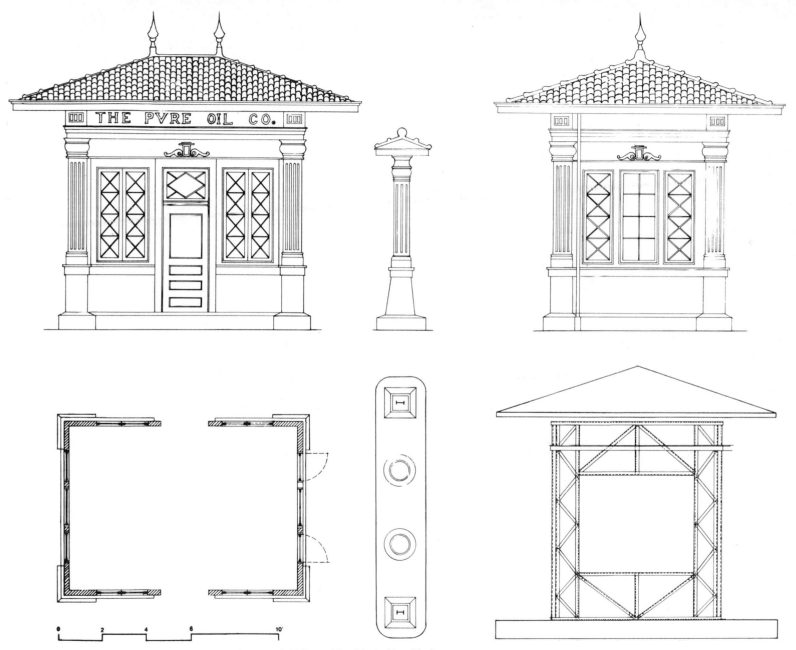

THE PVRE OIL CO.

0   2   4   6   10'

Fig. 104   Drawings of 1920s station model, Greenwich Village, New York, New York

stations. To date, most of the stations receiving attention have been of the Fantastic type. Milwaukee, for example, has designated a remaining Wadham Oil Company pagoda station as a local landmark (see Chapter 2, Fig. 31). Teepees, icebergs, airplanes, and Chinese pagodas are among the more flamboyant stations that statewide surveys have revealed as part of the continuing nationwide effort to identify historic resources.

The National Register of Historic Places, a prestigious listing of districts, sites, structures, and objects significant in American history, architecture, and culture, includes several gas stations. Listed as individual structures or as part of districts, these stations have taken their place alongside buildings like Mount Vernon and Independence Hall. The nomination statement of the Fantastic shell-shaped station (see Chapter 2, Fig. 24) in Winston-Salem, North Carolina, describes the building as a "rare and unusual survival of early twentieth century [architecture] . . . an example of the vernacular roots from which pop architecture grew . . . [it] merits recognition and preservation." Among the Fantastic natural wonders, one finds a station that is an integral part of Lemmon, South Dakota's Petrified Park. Constructed in 1929 from petrified logs and stones dating from Mesozoic times, the station has been converted to house the chamber of commerce. The Fantastic E. W. Norris service station in Kansas (see Chapter 2, Fig. 27) resembles a castle, and, according to its nomination, ". . . was then as now a unique architectural conception of a filling station."

A 1920s prefabricated classical pavilion model, one of many units purchased by the Pure Oil Company and manufactured by the Edwards Manufacturing Company of Cincinnati, Ohio, features elaborate ornamentation embossed in the station's pressed-metal walls. One of these (presently, Getty Oil) Respectable stations located in Greenwich Village, New York, has been nominated for inclusion on the National Register.

The results of pioneering efforts at standardization of Domestic stations have been given national recognition. The Pure Oil Company station in Saratoga Springs, New York, is part of a National Register district.

A "Functional" brick box (a Magnolia Company station) in Fayetteville, Arkansas, once housed a local company's retail outlet. Made of cream-colored brick with green trim, the station appears on the National Register.

Recognition of a gas station's cultural and architectural value provides the impetus for its preservation, either through rehabilitation and restoration or through adaptive reuse. The purest form of preservation involves restoration of a building on its original site. As with other historic buildings, however, gas stations must sometimes be moved to be preserved. When the original use is no longer viable, preservation involves the introduction of new functions. This adaptive reuse gives the building a new lease on life.

Examples of preservation or rehabilitation of stations to continue serving their original function are relatively rare. A recent significant case involved a Respectable (see Chapter 3), neoclassical Gulf station in Washington, DC. One of several identical stations built in 1936 in harmony with the federal neoclassical architecture as well as embassies and ecclesiastic structures, the impressive limestone edifice features classical columns, arched windows, and pedimented, gabled roofs. In 1973, Gulf announced plans to demolish the building and replace it with a modern structure. Later that year, the oil company, after discussions with neighbors and the city's Commission on Fine Arts, chose to renovate the structure.

Sometimes, preservation necessitates relocating the station itself. The Fantastic teapot station (see Chapter 2, page 18), built near Zillah, Washington, in the aftermath of the Harding administration's Teapot Dome scandal, has been moved to make way for a superhighway and is scheduled for restoration at the new site. The Pure Oil Domestic cottage in New York, listed on the National Register, sold for five hundred dollars, with the provision that it be moved to create space for a convention center. When put in its new location, one mile from its original site, this station, with its bay picture window and quaint character, will be recycled as commercial offices.

The idea of adaptive reuse is not new to service stations; in fact, many early gas stations or garages were converted from other uses. As mentioned in Chapter 2, a Tarrytown, New York, inn on the Boston Post Road became the Fantastic Headless Horseman station. The small lounges, with their wood-burning fireplaces, on the ground floor lend themselves to accommodating motorists, while the upstairs is an apartment for the station manager.

In the early days of this century, blacksmith shops began selling petroleum. As the demand for the smithy's art declined, a blacksmith shop in Montana was converted to a filling station–auto repair shop. Where horses once trotted through the metaphoric horseshoe opening to be reshod, the automobile now drives through to be refueled. Also originally geared to the horse, carriage houses and stables often converted to automobile service centers. A "Functional" Sunoco station in Westchester, New York, originally a wooden carriage house, now bears a gleaming porcelain enamel billboardlike façade that dwarfs the original structure.

Sometimes only key elements are preserved before the building is demolished. These features then find application in new construction. As seen in an earlier chapter, the Gabriel Manigault mansion (Charleston, South Carolina), dating from about 1800, provided the architectural elements for an Exxon service station. Created from the mansion's remains, this 1920s Respectable station incorporates Ionic columns, elegant windows with trim, and a fancy balustrade in its design.

Adaptive reuse involving the conversion from gas stations to other functions is the most prevalent form of station preservation. Edward Koren's 1978 *New Yorker* cartoon illustrates the fashionable nature of gas station reuse by portraying a cocktail party at which one person proclaims, "We live a few miles from here in an architecturally significant former gas station." Early stations in particular are often too small to continue functioning efficiently. Often the underground

Fig. 105 Washington, DC

Fig. 106 Westchester County, New York

Fig. 107 Charleston, South Carolina

fuel tanks are too small and the building can no longer house up-to-date technical equipment. In other cases, changing traffic patterns have rendered the location economically unfeasible for gasoline distribution. Moreover, the energy crisis has resulted in a reduction of petroleum outlets. In the five years following the Arab oil embargo, as many as ten thousand stations closed each year.

In a drive-in culture such as ours (of which the gasoline station was perhaps the earliest manifestation) a variety of other uses for former filling stations are possible. Albert L. Kerth, an architect who designed and supervised the construction of Getty Oil stations for twenty-eight years, recently wrote a book entitled *New Life for the Abandoned Service Station*. Prompted by the vision of twelve closed stations on a three-mile stretch of road, Kerth suggests ninety-seven alternate uses for filling stations and presents many conceptual drawings.

A series of compelling economic arguments for the adaptive reuse of abandoned stations exists. Evidence of a company's failure, an empty station is viewed by the larger corporations as a significant liability. These embarrassing eyesores then become available at attractive prices. Usually found in prime business locations, abandoned stations frequently offer large sites allowing for adequate parking. Perhaps most importantly, conversion is quicker than new construction, and since the properties are already zoned for commercial uses, potential problems regarding zoning changes can be avoided.

The uses of these converted stations range from the ad hoc to the sophisticated, from auto repair shops to elegant restaurants to prestige offices. The more spontaneous reuses involve services still related directly to the automobile. Audio centers specializing in automobile radios and CB equipment make use of the service bays for installations. Tire centers and repair shops also use some of the station's original features. Car rental agencies and used-car lots make use of interior service areas as well as the spacious, unencumbered lots for the storage and display of automobiles. An old gas station in Rochester, New York, houses a fire company.

KOREN

"We live a few miles from here in an architecturally significant former gas station."

Fig. 108
Drawing by
Edward Koren

Branch banks exploit the drive-in nature of the gas station. They sometimes refit the pump islands with technically advanced remote-teller units. The Coolidge Bank in Cambridge, Massachusetts, provides a particularly striking example of station reuse, as undertaken by the well-known preservation architectural firm of Anderson, Notter and Finegold. In many conversions, the Respectable station has proven almost ideal; it already projects the image deemed desirable for a bank.

Fig. 109   Houston, Texas

Fig. 110
Wappingers Falls,
New York

Fig. 111
Beacon,
New York

Fig. 112 Fishkill, New York

Fig. 113 Houston, Texas

Figs. 114 & 115 Houston, Texas

Other adaptive reuses take advantage of some or all of the general business considerations, including location on traffic arteries, adequate parking on site, and spacious interiors provided by the gutted service bays. Some convenience-goods stores feature tobacco, beer, and assorted groceries instead of tires, batteries, and accessories. Once the "mom and pop" grocery added gasoline to its wares; in this adaptive reuse, groceries return, supplementing or even replacing gasoline.

Roadside eateries, ranging from small doughnut shops to elegant restaurants, exist in former gas station facilities. Easily adapted, the large expanses of space in these buildings house kitchen machinery as well as dining facilities. Across the country, Mr. Donut, a division of International Multifoods Corporation, has rehabilitated several gasoline stations. Still other uses, which place machinery in the large spaces, include cleaners and laundromats. Stations have been converted for such diverse uses as a porno movie house in Southfield, Michigan, and a Baptist church in Springfield, Missouri. Many retail outlets and small commercial offices enjoy the station's flexible interior open space as well as its easily accessible parking.

Real estate offices housed in Domestic stations use the station's image to best advantage. A ranch-house-style gas station in Houston, Texas, originally an exaggerated restatement of its residential surroundings, now provides the headquarters for the brokers of nearby homes. This reuse retains as many of the station's image-projecting features as possible. The three garage doors leading to the grease racks have yielded to small, paned bay windows which reveal an elegant office. Looking like a living room, the main office features wooden fans suspended from the cathedral ceilings, antique rosewood furniture, and parquet floors accented by oriental rugs. This ensemble creates the perfect atmosphere to discuss the purchase of an exclusive Houston home.

As one critic of the gas station population problem stated, "Old gas stations never die, they are born again." Successful rebirth involves the incorporation of the station's most prominent characteristic—its image—into the new form.

The supply of gasoline station structures is so abundant that it is possible they will outlive our supply of gasoline. Under new forces of austerity, where not every station offers a full range of services, will today's marketing of gasoline revert to the cruder, sometimes naïve, images that characterized initial petroleum marketing? Or will the return to a simpler station, overlayed with the imprint of a large corporation, create a new image of station design?

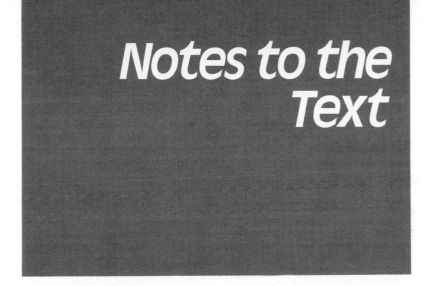

Introduction

(p. xiii)   carscape

PETER BLAKE, *God's Own Junkyard: The Planned Deterioration of America's Landscape* (New York: Holt, Rinehart and Winston, 1964), pp. 119 ff.

(p. xiii)   motorscape

DANIEL J. BOORSTEIN, editor's preface to: John B. Rae, *The American Automobile: A Brief History* (Chicago: University of Chicago Press, 1965), pp. vii–viii.

(p. xiii)   "The history of architecture must not be confined to master-pieces. . . . The subject is much bigger and comprises all that man has done . . . to shape the environment."

BRUCE ALLSOP, *The Study of Architectural History* (New York: Praeger Publishers, 1970), pp. 118–119.

(p. xiv)   "The combination of strict functionalism and bold symbolism in the best roadside stands provides, perhaps, the most encouraging sign for the architecture of the mid-twentieth century."

HENRY-RUSSELL HITCHCOCK, *The Architecture of H. H. Richardson and His Times* (Cambridge, Mass.: MIT Press, 1936), pp. 302–303.

(p. xiv)   Not until the 1960s did architects and theorists deal with the importance of the gas station

ROBERT VENTURI, DENISE SCOTT BROWN, "A Significance For A & P Parking Lots, Or Learning From Las Vegas," *The Architectural Forum* 128, no. 3 (March 1968), p. 36 ff. This was followed by a full-length book from which the article was excerpted: ROBERT VENTURI, DENISE SCOTT BROWN, and STEVEN IZENOUR, *Learning From Las Vegas* (Cambridge, Mass.: MIT Press, 1972)./Charles Moore in making a plea for an "architecture of inclusion" acknowledged the importance of road-side building in: "Plug It In, Rameses, and See if Its Lights Up: Because We Aren't Going to Keep It Unless It Works," *Perspecta II* (New Haven: Yale School of Architecture, 1967).

(p. xiv)   David Gebhard has played a vital role

An analysis of our drive-in culture's importance is presented by DAVID GEBHARD in "The Moderne in the U.S. 1920–1941," *Architectural Association Quarterly* 2 (July 1970), pp. 4–20, originally presented as: DAVID GEBHARD and HARRIETTE VON BRETON, *Kem Weber—The Moderne in Southern California, 1920 through 1941* (Santa Barbara: The Art Galleries, University of California, 1969)./Gebhard's *LA in*

the Thirties: 1931–1941 (Santa Barbara: Peregrine Smith, 1975) acknowledges the role of the automobile in Los Angeles's development.

Other works dealing with the architecture of gas stations have been undertaken. Among them are:

- American Society of Planning Officials, Planning Advisory Service, *The Design, Regulation, & Location of Service Stations.* Report Number 293, July/August 1973.
- "Money to be Made: The Oil Marketing Story, A Quick History of Oil Marketing," *National Petroleum News* (February 1969), pp. 111–134.
- WARREN C. PLATT, "Competition: Invited by the Nature of the Oil Industry," *National Petroleum News* (February 5, 1936), pp, 202–216.
- ITALO WILLIAM RICCIUTI, "Garages and Service Stations," Chapter 44 in Volume 4 of Talbot Hamlin's *Forms and Functions of Twentieth Century Architecture* (New York: Columbia University Press, 1952).
- GERALD T. LITTLEFIELD, *A History, Development and Analysis of Service Stations in the United States.* (Unpublished research paper, Columbia University, 1948).
- K. LONBERG-HOLM, "The Gasoline Filling and Service Station," *Architectural Record* 67, no. 6 (June 1930), pp. 561–583.
- "Service Stations: *Architectural Record*'s Building Types Study #86," *Architectural Record* 95, no. 2 (February 1944), pp. 71–92, 120, 122.
- ROLF VAHLEFELD and FRIEDRICH JACQUES, *Garages and Service Stations* (London: Leonard Hill Books Limited, 1960 [orig. 1953]).
- GARY HERBERT WOLF, *The Gasoline Station: The Evolution of a*

Building Type as Illustrated Through a History of the Sun Oil Company Gasoline Station. (Unpublished thesis, University of Virginia, 1974).

1 Beginnings

(p. 3) assembly-line production methods

On September 21, 1893, the American street saw its first internal combustion automobile—a creation of the Duryea Brothers based on a description of Benz's car published in *Scientific American.* In 1908 Henry Ford produced 5,986 Model Ts, offering them to the public for $850 each. By 1916, with 577,036 Model Ts on the road, the retail price had been brought down to $360. JOHN B. RAE, *The American Automobile: A Brief History* (Chicago: University of Chicago Press, 1965), pp. 9 and 61 respectively.

(p. 3) "Why, you can't go to town in a bathtub!"

ERNEST R. MAY and *Life* editors, *War, Boom and Bust, Volume 10: 1917–1932* (New York: Time Inc., 1974), p. 78./The flavor of the early automotive era is captured in DAVID L. COHN's *Combustion on Wheels* (Boston: Houghton Mifflin, 1944).

(p. 3) what had been a waste product of the kerosene industry

In 1899 virtually all of the 6.2 million barrels of gasoline were used for cleaning, heating, or lighting. By 1919, 85 percent of the 87.5 million barrels produced went to automobiles. HAROLD F. WILLIAMSON, RALPH L. ANDREWS, ARNOLD R. DAUM, and GILBERT C. KLOSE, *The American Petroleum Industry: The Age of Energy 1899–1959* (Evanston, Ill.: Northwestern University Press, 1963), pp. 194–195.

(p. 4) as early as 1905 . . . C. H. Laessig. . . .

WARREN C. PLATT, "Competition Invited by the Nature of the Oil Industry," *National Petroleum News* (February 5, 1936), p. 205.

(p. 4) introduction of gas pump is credited to Sylvanius F. Bowser

"Pump's Progress—The Tower to Match the Power," *Texaco Dealer* (February 1958), pp. 8–10./G. RICHARD MINNICK, "The Silent Sentinel of the American Road—Part I," *Antique Automobile* (January 1964), pp. 17–27.

(p. 7) "It takes but few minutes to get in, fill the tank. . . ."

"Station for Autoists—St. Louis Oil Company Puts in Down Town Plant for Consumers," *National Petroleum News* (May 1910), as cited

in WARREN C. PLATT, "Competition Invited by the Nature of the Oil Industry," *National Petroleum News* (February 5, 1936), p. 205.

(p. 7) national highway system not yet established

"The automobile won't get anywhere until it has good roads to run on. Why can't we build a highway from New York to San Francisco?" asked automotive enthusiast CARL GRAHAM FISHER. With that he began organizing the first serious attempt to build good roads: The Lincoln Highway Association. CHRISTY BORTH, *Mankind on the Move: The Story of Highways* (Washington, DC: Automotive Safety Foundation, 1969), pp. 184–186./This private organization terminated its work when the Federal Road Act of 1916 "offered a prospect of obtaining an effective national highway system." JOHN B. RAE, *The American Automobile: A Brief History* (Chicago: University of Chicago Press, 1965), pp. 51–52.

(p. 7) The solution? prefabricated gas stations

Advertisement of the Metal Shelter Company, St. Paul, Minnesota, *National Petroleum News* (August 26, 1926), p. 92.

(p. 7) split pump stations sold several brands of gasoline

"Country Station Sells Seven Gasolines," *National Petroleum News* (November 20, 1929), p. 80.

(p. 8) brand loyalties had to be instilled among consumers

"Almost Half of Motorists Buy a Brand, Marketing Survey Finds," *National Petroleum News* (April 25, 1928), p. 27./"Expansion of national crude oil production . . . led producing companies to do their utmost to stake out claims on the loyalty of motorists at almost any cost." MELVIN DE CHAZEAU and ALFRED KAHN, *Integration and Competition in the Petroleum Industry* (New Haven: Yale University Press, 1959), pp. 114–115.

(p. 14) station attendants in uniforms

V. B. GUTHRIE, "Motorists tell in Their Own Words What They Expect at Filling Stations," *National Petroleum News* (November 17, 1926), p. 92.

(p. 14) a credit card system had its beginnings as a gasoline purchasing convenience

DANIEL J. BOORSTIN, *The Americans: The Democratic Experience* (New York: Random House, 1973), p. 427.

(p. 15)   stations took the form of single-propeller airplanes

Airplane Gulf station. Gulf Oil Corporation Archives. (No location, no date). Skelly station #2, Topeka, Kansas. Letter from Kansas Historical Society (June 12, 1978).

(p. 15)   airplane stations

Independent Retailer, Magnolia, Arkansas.

(p. 15)   1929 galleon station

"Seashore Gasoline Station Modeled After Ship," *National Petroleum News* (June 19, 1928), p. 112.

(p. 17)   lighthouse stations

A chain of five Cities Service lighthouse stations was opened in Delaware. "Portable Country Stations Are Replicas of Famous Lighthouse," *National Petroleum News* (September 26, 1928), p. 68./A modest stucco lighthouse station survives in Quincy, Massachusetts.

(p. 17)   Socony-Mobil "lighthouse"

"These Socony Outlets Won First Awards In Long Island Civic Group's Contest," *Socony-Vacuum Flash* (March 20, 1933), p. 1.

(p. 17)   at the entrance to Miami Beach

Station by Polevitzky and Russell, architects. "To Enjoy Nature We Need Commerce," *Architectural Record* 89, no. 4, (April 1941), pp. 84–85.

(p. 17)   Gallon Measure service station

Interview with Mr. Ray Gallaher, builder and original proprietor of Gallon Measure service station, Buchanan, New York (June 23, 1976).

(p. 18)   sleeping loft

Sleeping lofts in stations not only made it practical for a station to be open twenty-four hours a day but reduced insurance premiums since a constantly occupied station was given a different classification. H. ROGER GRANT, "Highway Commercial Architecture: Albia, Iowa's Dutch Mill," *The Palimpsest* 58, no. 3 (Iowa State Historical Department: May/June 1977), p. 86.

(p. 18)   replica of a tank car

"Station Modeled After Tank Car," *National Petroleum News* (November 12, 1930), p. 205.

(p. 18)   station made to look like an oil derrick

H. ROGER GRANT, "Highway Commercial Architecture: Albia, Iowa's Dutch Mill," *The Palimpsest* 58, no. 3 (May/June 1977), p. 84.

(p. 18)   station modeled after a teapot

"Teapot to be fixed, moved," *Tri-City Herald*, Pasco, Washington (August 17, 1977), p. 1.

(p. 18)   shell-shaped Shell station

"Shell Quality Oil Company, Winston-Salem, North Carolina," *National Petroleum News* (February 25, 1931), p. 69./BRENT GLASS, MARY ALICE HINSON, National Register of Historic Places, inventory-nomination form for Shell service station, Winston-Salem, North Carolina (October 30, 1975).

(p. 18)   shell-shaped travel and tourist pavilion

Advertisement for Independent Iron Works, Oakland, California, *The Architect and Engineer* 123, no. 1 (October 1935), p. 1.

(p. 19)   Dino the Dinosaur

"Updating the Service Station Image," *Industrial Design* 12, no. 8 (August 1965), p. 44.

(p. 20)   "Only Petrified Wood Filling Station"

Postcard of the "only petrified wood filling station in the world," W. G. Brown, builder and owner, Lamar, Colorado.

(p. 20)   "World's Largest Petrified Wood Park"

SCOTT GERLOFF, National Register of Historic Places nominating form for Lemmon Petrified Park, Lemmon, South Dakota (1975).

(p. 20)   Madonna Inn

CHARLES MOORE, "Plug It in, Ramses, and See if It Lights Up: Because We Aren't Going to Keep It Unless It Works," *Perspecta II* (New Haven: Yale School of Architecture, 1967), p. 43.

(p. 20) giant icebergs

Letter from Kansas Historical Society (June 12, 1978).

(p. 20) eatery–filling station in the form of a southern mammy

Often photographed, the station caught the attention of photographer Edward Weston while on his 1941 trip in search of illustrations for a special edition of Whitman's classic *Leaves of Grass*. Editors of Time-Life Books, *Life Library of Photography: Great Photographers*, 1971, p. 174.

(p. 20) Headless Horseman Texaco station

"Station Revives Ichabod Crane's Love Affair," *National Petroleum News* (August 28, 1929), p. 88.

(p. 21) thoroughly defensible medieval castle

RICHARD PANKRATZ, National Register of Historic Places, inventory-nomination form for E. W. Norris service station, Glen Elder, Kansas, 1976.

(p. 22) "Eat and Sleep in a Wigwam"

"Eat & Sleep in a Wigwam," *Standard Oil Retailer*. Courtesy of Library of Congress. Photo by Marion Post Wolcott, July 1940.

(p. 22) premier example of the wigwam phenomenon

Lawrence, Kansas station, LOUIS WELLER, "Indian Village to Grow Around Station," *National Petroleum News* (June 25, 1930), p. 89ff.

(p. 22) windmill station in Holland, Michigan

Vandembury Brothers Oil Company. *National Petroleum News* (August 1925).

(p. 22) windmill station in Schenectady, New York

C. F. Williams and Company. *National Petroleum News* (December 18, 1929), p. 90.

(p. 22) windmill station in Macomb, Illinois

KEITH A. SCULLE, "Four Gas Stations from a Golden Era," *Illinois Magazine* (August/September 1978), p. 70.

(p. 22) windmill stations in Iowa

Old Dutch Windmill station. A. Pilicer, proprietor. *National Petroleum News* (March 4, 1925), p. 70./Dutch Mill Service Company, H. Gholson, proprietor: Chain of stations with outlets in Knoxville, Charlton, Leon, Corydon, and Albia, Iowa. *National Petroleum News* (March 19, 1930), p. 124./H. ROGER GRANT, "Highway Commercial Architecture: Albia, Iowa's Dutch Mill," *The Palimpsest* (May/June 1977), p. ff.

(p. 23) pyramids of Egypt

"Egypt Dictates Service Station Style," *National Petroleum News* (March 9, 1932), p. 44.

(p. 23) Wadham's Oil and Grease Company, Wisconsin

WAYNE ATTOE and MARK LATUS, "Buildings as Signs: An Experiment in Milwaukee," *Popular Architecture*, edited by J. M. NEILL & MARSHALL FISHWICK, The Popular Press, Bowling Green, Ohio, 1975, pp. 84–87./WAYNE ATTOE and MARK LATUS, "Orient Inspires First Gasoline Stations," Home Section, *Milwaukee Journal* (February 8, 1973), p. 1./Harley Sprague Station: MARK A. LATUS, Wisconsin Inventory of Historic Places, 1973. MARK A. LATUS, MARY ELLEN YOUNG, Milwaukee County Directory of Historic Places, 1973.

(p. 24) Power Plus station

National Petroleum News photo (March 15, 1923).

(p. 24) Mobile, Alabama, station built for the Huxford Oil Company

Mobile Historic Development Commission.

(p. 25) prefabricated oriental-style stations

Model produced by the Edwards Manufacturing Company, Cincinatti, Ohio. Advertisement in *National Petroleum News* (March 20, 1929).

(p. 25) "oriental" Texaco station

The Texaco Star 17, no. 3 (March 30), rear cover.

(p. 25) Calpet station's lush decor

"An Auto Service Station; ROLAND E. COATE, Architect," *Architectural Record* 63, no. 4 (April 1928), pp. 302–304./"Super Station Designed as Mosque," *National Petroleum News* (April 18, 1928), p. 93ff.

(p. 25) In Washington, DC . . . a station for the Columbia Oil Company

HORACE W. PEASLEE, architect./ ALEXANDER G. GUTH, "The Automobile Service Station," *The Architectural Forum* 45, no. 1 (July 1926), pp. 45–46.

(p. 27) Grant's Tomb

"Service Station Field is Playground for Architectural Design," *National Petroleum News* (May 13, 1925), p. 72.

(p. 27) "the service station can be made a civic asset"

LUCY LOWE, "Service Stations as an Asset to the City," *The American City* 25, no. 2 (August 1921), p. 153.

(p. 27) City Beautiful movement in America

MEL SCOTT, *American City Planning Since 1890* (Berkeley: University of California Press, 1971), pp. 47–109.

(p. 27) City Beautiful movement linked civic beauty to a variety of concerns

JON A. PETERSON, "The City Beautiful Movement: Forgotten Origins and Lost Meanings," *Journal of Urban History* 2, no. 4 (August 1976) pp. 415–434.

(p. 27) "Filling stations were not . . . matters of civic pride"

LUCY LOWE, "Service Stations as an Asset to the City," *The American City* 25, no. 2 (August 1921), p. 51.

(p. 27) "Streets throughout the entire country are littered by horrible examples of poorly designed filling stations."

H. T. FROST, "Prize-Winning Designs in the Biscayne Boulevard Competitions," *The American City* 35, no. 6 (December 1926), p. 837.

(p. 28) "dedicated to the goddess of internal combustion. . . ."

Station by J. F. Kuntz of the architectural firm of W. G. Wilkens Company, Pittsburgh, Pennsylvania. J. F. KUNTZ, "Greek Architecture and Gasoline Service Stations," *The American City* 27, no. 2 (August 1922), pp. 123–124./Station photographed in *Your New Filling Station*, National Terra Cotta Society.

(p. 28) prefabricated metal and glass buildings

Advertisement for the Edwards Manufacturing Company, Cincinnati, Ohio. *National Petroleum News* (October 23, 1929), p. 105.

(p. 29) station paraphernalia

Advertisement for station accessories produced by the Union Metal Manufacturing Company of Canton, Ohio. *National Petroleum News* (March 11, 1925), p. 19./Advertisement for "America's Finest Visible Pump," *National Petroleum News* (August 26, 1925), rear cover.

(p. 29) domed Beacon stations

Among the locations were: Dorchester, Massachusetts—ALEXANDER G. GUTH, "The Automobile Service Station," *The Architectural Forum* 45, no. 1 (July 1926), colonial filling station #27, pp. 47–48; Englewood, New Jersey—Mobil Oil Corporation Photo Library, November 2, 1944; Somerville, Massachusetts. *National Petroleum News* (May 13, 1925), p. 134; Stoneham, Massachusetts. Photo by RICHARD J. S. GUTMAN, 1976.

(p. 29) structures built in the Spanish mode

The San Diego Panama California Exposition of 1916, a Spanish colonial extravaganza, gave the style an impetus just as classical styles had been popularized by the 1893 World's Columbian Exposition in Chicago. See *The Architecture and the Gardens of the San Diego Exposition* (Paul Elder and Company, San Francisco, 1916), with an introduction by BERTRAM GROSVENOR GOODHUE, Advisory and Consulting Architect of the Exposition. A more recent discussion of the style is presented by DAVID GEBHARD's "The Spanish Colonial Revival in Southern California (1895–1930)," *Journal of the Society of Architectural Historians* 26, no. 2 (May 1967), pp. 131–147.

(p. 30) Union Oil Company of California sponsored a competition

The results of the Union Oil Company of California service station competition were published in two architectural journals: "Winners of Gasoline Filling Station Competition," *The Architect and Engineer* 92, no. 1 (January 1928), pp. 100–101; "Union Oil Company of California Service Station Competition," *The American Architect* 133 (March 5, 1928), pp. 331–333.

(p. 30) a standard design for the Southwest

"The Modern Service Station," *National Petroleum News* (March 19, 1930)./"1931 Trends in Station Designs," *National Petroleum News* (March 4, 1931), p. 98.

(p. 31) the destruction of the Gabriel Manigault mansion

"Business and Preservation. Exxon: A Case Study," *Preservation News* 16, no. 4 (April 1976), p. 7.

(p. 31) many other simple stations attached new, grand, decorative trim

A finely detailed door, fanlight, and sidelight, plus an elegant colonial window and balustrade gave Beacon Oil colonial filling station #54 in Dorchester, Massachusetts, its elegant appearance. ALEXANDER G. GUTH, "The Automobile Service Station," *The Architectural Forum* 45, no. 1 (July 1926). A majestic Palladian window was a prominent feature of a standardized model of the Standard Oil Company of New York.

(p. 32) pedimented portico

Station of the Cities Service Oil Co., Cleveland, Ohio. "The Modern Service Station," *National Petroleum News* (March 19, 1930), p. 133./ Station of the Lincoln Oil Company, Vincennes, Indiana. "Lincoln One-Stop Station Fits In With 'Beautify the Community' Campaign," *National Petroleum News* (March 4, 1931), p. 4.

(p. 33) counterpart to the classical porch

J. B. Lafourcade gas station, Cucamonga, California./ "Builds Station to Help Reclaim Desert," *National Petroleum News* (July 18, 1928), p. 84.

(p. 33) bell tower

Harold Snyder Super-Service Station, Oklahoma City, Oklahoma. "Oklahoma City Station Provides Phone Service at Gas Pump," *National Petroleum News* (November 2, 1932), p. 36. Presently Safeway Cab Company.

(p. 33) service centers . . . along the Pacific coast's highways

Each station was to be made visible for fifty miles by a 125-foot neon beacon. This tower was a restatement of the structure crowning Richfield's newly finished (1928) Los Angeles headquarters, designed by Morgan, Walls & Clements (1928). This building is discussed in DAVID GEBHARD's monograph *The Richfield Building: 1928–1968* (Los Angeles: Atlantic Richfield Co., 1970); "Beacon Towers for Flyers at Richfield Stations," *National Petroleum News* (June 5, 1929), p. 103; A chain of stations was planned as part of roadside "communities," offering services to the traveler; W. E. GREEN, "Chain Stations De Luxe By Highways, Are California Venture," *National Petroleum News* (August 22, 1928), p. 25; California prototype by Wilson & Merrill, architects, Los Angeles, California; "The Modern Service Station," *National Petroleum News* (March 19, 1930), p. 117; "Motor Fuel Stations in Variety," *Architecture* 63, no. 2 (February 1931), p. 80; "Four Service Stations," *American Architecture* 142 (November 1932), p. 55; Station near the Canadian border conveys the image of a chalet

snow lodge; K. LONBERG-HOLM, "The Gasoline Filling and Service Station," *The Architectural Record* 67, no. 6 (June 1930), p. 564.

(p. 34) hacienda-style station

Ray Roger's Mobil station, San Antonio, Texas (1977).

(p. 34) a Gulf station in Washington, DC

J. Y. SMITH, "NW Gas Station Will be Preserved," *The Washington Post* (April 27, 1973).

(p. 35) reduced . . . to a few vestigial elements

Gulf Oil station, Pittsburgh, Pennsylvania, 1955. Gulf Oil Corp. archives.

(p. 36) Shell station designed in 1932

Romanesque station near Stanford University, H. O. ALDEN, Architect. L. RAYMOND WHITE, "Oil Stations," *The Architect and Engineer* 123, no. 1 (October 1935), p. 32. Shell Oil Company photograph, 1935.

(p. 36) collegiate Gothic forms

C. Gianacaci Gulf station, Princeton, New Jersey.

(p. 36) Sherman Oaks service station in Van Nuys, California

"Automobile Service Stations," *Architecture* 72, no. 2 (August 1935), p. 101.

(p. 39) San Francisco headquarters

"How Shell Modernizes Its West Coast Station Buildings," *National Petroleum News* (September 21, 1932), pp. 41–44./ Shell Oil Company service station, San Francisco, California. Shell Oil Company photograph, 1931.

(p. 40) station . . . adjacent to its new headquarters

PETER C. PAPADEMETRIOU, "As Modern As 1948," *Architectural Design* 41, no. 3 (March 1971), pp. 132–133.

4 The Domestic

(p. 41) "If they were once too weird. . . ."

"Filling Stations for Town Betterment," *House and Garden* 47, no. 6 (June 1925), p. 44.

(p. 41) Picturesque movement

Perhaps the most comprehensive examination of the Picturesque movement is found in CHRISTOPHER HUSSEY's *The Picturesque: Studies in a Point of View* (London: Frank Cass & Co., 1927; Hamden, Conn.: Anchor Books, 1967).

(p. 41) "In the most beautiful parts of the country, the scenery is disfigured. . . ."

PETER FREDERICK ROBINSON, *Rural Architecture: or a Series of Designs for Ornamental Cottages* (London: Rodwell and Martin, 1823), [p. i.]

(p. 41) "No one passing at less than forty miles an hour could fail to notice this unusual bit of architecture."

Spindler filling & service station, Manitowoc, Wisconsin, CHARLES CLARKE REYNOLDS, architect. ALEXANDER G. GUTH, "The Automobile Service Station," *The Architectural Forum* 45, no. 1 (July 1926), pp. 41–42.

(p. 41) the characteristically irregular forms of these gas stations

A number of picturesque cottage stations were published in ALEXANDER G. GUTH's, "The Automobile Service Station," *The Architectural Forum*. Among them were: Barkhausen Oil Company station, Green Bay, Wisconsin, CLARENCE O. JOHN, designer; Waupun Oil Company station, Waupun, Wisconsin, CLARENCE O. JOHN, designer; Bartles-McGuire Oil Company stations, Milwaukee, Wisconsin, (three different designs) BUEMMING & GUTH, architects.

(p. 42) ". . . how brands may be brought to the attention of the motorist without detracting from the orderly appearance of the station."

Station of the Pure Oil Company at Binghamton, New York. *National Petroleum News* (April 25, 1978), p. 27.

(p. 42) Sun Oil Company also produced a series of Domestic stations

Standard Sun Oil "cottage," Philadelphia, Pennsylvania. Sun Oil Company photograph./Later, slightly modified prototype in Ardmore,

Pennsylvania. "1931 Trends In Station Design," *National Petroleum News* (March 4, 1931), p. 89.

(p. 45) Whitehall filling station in Kansas City, Missouri

Whitehall filling station, Kansas City, Missouri, MADORIE & BIHR, architects. *The Architect* 12 (July 1929), pp. 451–453. Photo in Mobil Oil Corporation archives, New York. 1920–1929 scrapbook.

(p. 45) the addition of irregularly shaped buildings

"Housing the Grease Pit in Style," *National Petroleum News* (January 23, 1929), p. 72./"A Pure Oil Company Station Adapted to Two Service Wings," *National Petroleum News* (August 1, 1936)./Pure Oil Company station, Westerville, Ohio, 1937. Union 76 photograph.

(p. 45) tudor super-service stations

The first of many similar super-service stations of the Standard Oil Company of Ohio, this one in Cleveland, Ohio./N. M. MAINPA, "Speedy and Thorough Car Greasing Promised While Owner Watches," *National Petroleum News* (February 13, 1929), pp. 96–99./"Even Colors Picked to Help Sales at Ohio Standard's New Stations," *National Petroleum News* (June 5, 1929) pp. 94–98./Sinclair service station, Scarsdale, New York, W. STANWOOD PHILLIPS, architect. *American Architect* 146 (February 1935), pp. 48–49.

(p. 45) Radburn, New Jersey, the pioneering "city for the motor age"

MEL SCOTT, *American City Planning Since 1890* (Berkeley: University of California Press, 1971), p. 188./"New Town Planned for the Motor Age," *The American City* (February 1928), p. 152./"Construction Work Now Under Way for the Town of the Motor Age," *The American City* (October 1928), p. 81./HENRY M. PRAPPER, "Radburn's Unique Plan Shows Results," *The American City* 41, no. 5 (November 1929), pp. 142–144./"Gasoline Stations Become Architectural Assets," *The American City* 41, no. 5 (November 1929), p. 98./K. LONBERG-HOLM, "The Gasoline Filling and Service Station," *The Architectural Record* 67, no. 6 (June 1930), p. 583.

(p. 45) station suggested for adoption by a *House and Garden* of 1925

"Filling Stations for Town Betterment," *House and Garden* 47, no. 6 (June 1925), p. 95.

(p. 47) Dallas's 1931 Highland Park Village

Highland Park Shopping Village, Dallas, Texas. *Dallasights: An Anthropology of Architecture and Open Spaces* (American Institute of Architects, Dallas chapter), p. 36.

(*p. 49*) Highland Park station complemented the shopping complex

"The Modern Service Station," *National Petroleum News* (May 4, 1932), p. 33.

(*p. 49*) the parkway

GILMORE D. CLARKE, "Westchester Parkways, Modern Motor Ways," *The Architectural Record* 74, no. 12 (December 1933), pp. 430–436.

(*p. 49*) Westchester County Park Commission

"Gas Stations Become Architectural Assets," *The American City* 41, no. 5 (November 1929), p. 98./K. LONBERG-HOLM, "The Gasoline Filling and Service Station," *The Architectural Record* 67, no. 6 (June 1930), p. 583./"Four Service Stations," *American Architecture* 142 (November 1932), p. 56./"Automobile Service Stations," *Architecture* 72, no. 2 (August 1935), pp. 101–102./HAROLD HALIDAY COSTAIN, "Modern Gasoline Stations," *The Architectural Record* 90, no. 4 (October 1941), p. 69./Other parkway stations include: a station on the Westchester County Park Commission's Sawmill River Parkway by CLINTON LLOYD, architect, and GILMORE D. CLARKE, landscape architect; "Four Service Stations," *American Architecture* 142 (November 1932), p. 57./Stations on various parkways under the jurisdiction of the City of New York Department of Parks: "Filling Stations," *Pencil Points* 21, no. 4 (April 1940), pp. 231–232; "Gas Station at Jones Beach State Park, Long Island State Park Commission, New York," *The Architectural Record* 77, no. 5 (May 1935), pp. 354–55; "Filling Stations," *Pencil Points* 21, no. 1 (January 1941), pp. 35–40.

(*p. 50*) *Architecture* sponsored a competition

"*Architecture*'s Competition XI, Report of the Judges," *Architecture* 47, no. 3 (March 1928), p. 173–175.

(*p. 50*) "a credit to its neighborhood"

"This Station Hobnobs with a College," *National Petroleum News* (April 4, 1928), p. 31.

(*p. 50*) standard prototype, featuring colonial elements . . . pueblo counterpart

"Texaco Service Stations: A History," (unpublished manuscript, no date) Texaco archives, Texaco, Inc., New York, p. 3.

(*p. 51*) experimental prototypes developed

"A New Look In Filling Stations," *Industrial Design* 12, no. 1 (January 1965), pp. 54–55./"Updating The Service Station Image," *Industrial Design* 12, no. 8 (August 1965), pp. 46–47.

(*p. 53*) Lady Bird Johnson

"Soft Sell for Beauty," *Business Week* (February 19, 1966), p. 33./ STANLEY D. BREITWEISER, "An Oilman Talks Esthetics," *American Institute of Architects Journal* 46, no. 2 (August 1966), pp. 41–44.

(*p. 53*) conflicts that result from overlapping of styles

PETER C. PAPADEMETRIOU, "As Modern as 1948," *Architectural Design* 41, no. 3 (March 1971), pp. 132–133.

5 The "Functional"

(*p. 56*) "In recent years, a new type of station has made its appearance. . . ."

"Planning Techniques For New and Remodeled Buildings: Service Stations," *The Architectural Forum* 66, no. 2 (February 1937), p. 87.

(*p. 56*) "Good taste as well as cost. . . ."

ALEXANDER G. GUTH, "Small Buildings: The Automobile Service Station," *The Architectural Forum* 45, no. 1 (July 1926), p. 51.

(*p. 56*) celebrations of the technology that created them

The factorylike window walls of these stations call to mind ALBERT KAHN's early industrial architecture, especially his pioneering designs for automobile manufacturers: Packard Motor Car Company, Detroit, Michigan, 1903; Ford Motor Company, Highland Park Plant, 1909. See *The Legacy of Albert Kahn* (Detroit: Detroit Institute of Arts, 1970).

(*p. 56*) carefully groomed shrubbery and manicured flower beds

KENDALL BEATON, *Enterprise in Oil: A History of Shell in the United States* (New York: Appleton-Century-Crofts, 1957), p. 273./Associated Oil Company station, Portland, Oregon./"Station Building Set on Outside Corner," *National Petroleum News* (March 20, 1929), p. 112./K. LONBERG-HOLM, "The Gasoline Filling and Service Station," *The Architectural Record* 67, no. 6 (June 1930), p. 571./This concept was revived in the late sixties and seventies; often, however, "hardier" plastic plants were used. FRED A. ZIMMER, "Plastiche—The Living End," *Landscape Architecture* 62 (January 1972).

(*p. 56*) dual imagery carried over to the building itself

This was usually achieved by adorning the service drive canopy with elements reminiscent of a garden trellis. A standard model in use by the Gulf Oil Company in the late twenties exhibits this feature. "Fashion Show . . . in Service Station" (Pittsburgh: Gulf Oil Company, *no date*). Gulf Oil Company archives, Pittsburgh, Pennsylvania.

(p. 58)   inefficient, traditional ideas have been discarded

Ad insert for auto servitoriums by Truscon Steel Company, Youngstown, Ohio, *National Petroleum News* (August 10, 1932).

(p. 59)   introducing . . . modernism to the mainstream

HENRY-RUSSELL HITCHCOCK and PHILIP JOHNSON, *The International Style: Architecture Since 1922* (New York: W. W. Norton & Company, 1932).

(p. 59)   MOMA show of 1932 included a Standard Oil station

Standard Oil Company of Ohio station, CLAUSS & DAUB, architects. HENRY-RUSSELL HITCHCOCK and PHILIP JOHNSON, *The International Style: Architecture Since 1922* (New York: W. W. Norton & Company, 1932), pp. 112–113./"A Standardized Filling Station Unit," *The Architectural Record* 70, no. 6 (December 1931), p. 458.

(p. 59)   few examples of pure International Style buildings emerged in the United States

An analysis of why the International Style was not instantly accepted in this country is contained in a retrospective: ELIZABETH MOCK, ed., *Built in USA—Since 1932* (New York: Museum of Modern Art, distributed by Simon and Schuster, 1945), pp. 9–16.

(p. 59)   Yosemite National Park station

"Yosemite Service Station, ELDRIDGE T. SPENCER, Architect, San Francisco," *Pencil Points* 23, no. 1 (January 1942), pp. 43–46.

(p. 60)   "No one's driving enjoyment is increased. . . ."

WILLIAM LESCAZE, "On Being An Architect," *The Architectural Forum* 77, no. 9 (Septmber 1942), p. 16.

(p. 60)   ". . . use of fine, textured materials. . . ."

"Service Station, WILLIAM LESCAZE, Architect, New York," *The Architectural Forum* 77, no. 5 (May 1943), pp. 132–133.

(p. 60)   project . . . for Pittsburgh Plate Glass

"Service Station, ELY JACQUES KAHN, ROBERT ALLAN JACOBS, Architects," *Pencil Points* 25, no. 8 (August 1944), p. 53.

(p. 60)   designs constructed in Bakersfield, California

Prior to being awarded the commission for the Norwalk Oil Company station, Neutra had designed a home for the company's president. "Designing for the Motor Age: RICHARD NEUTRA and the Automobile." A lecture by THOMAS HINES at the Society Architectural Historians 1979 annual meeting, Savannah, Georgia./"Service Station, RICHARD J. NEUTRA, Architect," *Arts and Architecture* 65 (April 1948), p. 31./ RICHARD W. SNIBBE, *Small Commercial Buildings* (New York: Reinhold Publishing, 1956), pp. 102–103.

(p. 62)   Bertrand Goldberg's 1938 prototype

"Service Station is Hung from Masts to Minimize Foundations and Costs," *The Architectural Forum* 84, no. 3 (March 1946), p. 115./ RICHARD W. SNIBBLE, *Small Commercial Buildings* (New York: Reinhold Publishing, 1956), p. 101./STUART E. COHEN, *Chicago Architects* (Chicago: Swallow Press, 1976), pp. 24 and 88.

(p. 62)   Viennese-born RUDOLPH SCHINDLER's essays on service station design

1932 project for a Union Oil station "constructed of steel and glass and plants." DAVID GEBHARD and HARRIETTE VON BRETTON, *L.A. in the Thirties: 1931–1941* (Santa Barbara: Peregrine Smith, 1975), p. 61./1933 prototype service station for Union Oil Company, Los Angeles. "A Gasoline Station Design and Model by R. M. SCHINDLER, Architect," *The Architectural Record* 74, no. 8 (August 1933), pp. 142–144./1934 station for Mrs. Nerenbaum, probably Los Angeles. DAVID GEBHARD, *Schindler* (New York: Viking Press, 1971). All three station projects are mentioned briefly in this work.

(p. 63)   "The roadside service station. . . ."

FRANK LLOYD WRIGHT, *An Autobiography* (New York: Duell, Sloan and Pearce, 1943), p. 328.

(p. 63)   Broadacre City

BAKER BROWNELL, *Frank Lloyd Wright, Architecture and Modern Life* (New York: Harper & Brothers, 1937), p. 166./HENRY-RUSSELL HITCHCOCK, *In the Nature of Materials: The Buildings of Frank Lloyd Wright, 1887–1941* (New York: Hawthorn Books, 1942), pp. 80, 293, and 294.

(p. 63)   "How many trusties and lusties. . . ."

FRANK LLOYD WRIGHT, *An Autobiography* (New York: Duell, Sloan and Pearce, 1943), pp. 23–24.

(p. 64)   FRANK LLOYD WRIGHT designed a filling station for a Cloquet, Minnesota, retailer

ROBERT C. WHEELER, "Frank Lloyd Wright Filling Station, 1958," *Journal of the Society of Architectural Historians* 19, no. 4 (December 1960), pp. 174–175./DAVID GEBHARD and TOM MARTINSON, *A Guide to the Architecture of Minnesota* (Minneapolis: University of Minnesota Press, 1977), p. 186.

(p. 64)   the search for form of the 1950s

For a discussion of the influence on Wright of the International Style see: VINCENT J. SCULLY, JR., "Wright *vs.* the International Style," *ARTnews* 53, no. 1 (March 1954), pp. 32–35 and 64–66./PETER C. PAPADEMETRIOU, in his November 18, 1976, lecture "Shake, Rattle and van der Rohe" (part of the series: The Fifties From Eisenhower to Kennedy) at the Institute for Architecture and Urban Studies in New York, discussed the evolution of the 1950s search for form.

(p. 64)   soaring V-shaped canopy

"Updating the Service Station Image," *Industrial Design* 12, no. 8 (August 1965), pp. 42–49.

(p. 64)   epitomized by Carvel or the McDonald's of the fifties

"Service Station, Los Angeles, California, WILLIAM F. HEMPEL, Architect," *Progressive Architecture* 29, no. 1 (January 1948), pp. 91–93./ "Designed to Attract Attention, Wayne's Associated Service, Aiea, Oahu, T. H., WIMBERLY and COOK, Architects, J. GRANT MORGAN Structural Engineer," *The Architectural Record* 111, no. 6 (June 1952), pp. 185–187./"Erickson's Gas—Wisconsin & Minnesota, Prototype for a Chain of Service Stations, THORSHAW & CERNY, Architects, TED SUDANO, Architect In Charge," *The Architectural Record* 113, no. 5 (May 1953), p. 165./"Service Station, Harlingen, Texas, COCKE, BOWMAN & YORK, Architects and Engineers," *Progressive Architecture* 35, no. 9 (September 1954), pp. 106–107.

(p. 65)   Art Deco, or Moderne, paralleled the . . . technological expression of the modern movement

DONALD J. BUSH, *The Streamlined Decade* (New York: George Braziller, 1975)./DAVID GEBHARD and HARRIETTE VON BRETAN, *Kem Weber—The Moderne in Southern California, 1920 through 1941* (Santa Barbara: The Art Galleries, University of California, 1969)./ DAVID GEBHARD, "The Moderne in the US, 1920–1941," *Architectural Association Quarterly* 2 (July 1970), pp. 4–20./MARTIN GREIF, *Depression Modern: The Thirties Style in America* (New York: Universe Books, 1975)./BEVIS HILLIER, *Art Deco of the 20s and 30s* (New York: Dutton, 1968)./CERVIN ROBINSON and ROSEMARIE HAAG

BLETTER, *Skyscraper Style: Art Deco New York* (New York: Oxford University Press, 1975).

(p. 65)   Zig-zag Moderne was a contemporary idiom

Humble Oil & Refining standard station in use in Houston, Texas. "1931 Trends in Station Design," *National Petroleum News* (March 4, 1934), p. 87.

(p. 66)   Streamlined models of the 1930s and 1940s

Streamlining was evident in almost every entry in the "Automotive Sales and Service Station Competition sponsored by Libbey-Owens Ford Glass Company," *The Architectural Record* 78, no. 4 (October 1935), pp. 255–266.

(p. 66)   Streamlined design implemented by the Gulf Oil Company

Gulf station, Elmhurst, New York, 1939. "Fashion Show . . . Service Station Design," (Pittsburgh: Gulf Oil Company archives, no date).

(p. 67)   1934 Chrysler Airflow

The Chrysler Airflow was initially designed by CARL BREER and the Chrysler enginnering staff and later modified by NORMAN BEL GEDDES. DONALD J. BUSH, *The Streamlined Decade* (New York: George Braziller, 1975), pp. 119–120.

(p. 67)   NORMAN BEL GEDDES undertook a thorough study

KENNETH REID, "Master of Design 2: NORMAN BEL GEDDES," *Pencil Points* 18, no. 1 (January 1937), pp. 8–13.

(p. 69)   FREDERICK FROST, who developed a more conservative but visually exciting prototype

Mobil Oil station, FREDERICK G. FROST, Mobil Oil Corporation, Photo Library, New York./HENRY OZANNE, "Merchandizing Will Shape New Stations—*Architectural Record*'s Building Types Study Number 86," *The Architectural Record* 95, no. 2 (February 1944), p. 73./"Service Station, the Firm of Frederick G. Frost, Consulting Architects for Socony Vacuum Oil Co., Inc.," *Pencil Points* 26, no. 7 (July 1945), p. 82.

(p. 69)   Loewy's compact "Servicenter"

"Products and practice . . . constantly find new solutions for old problems. The high cost of corner plots for filling stations was one." *The Architectural Forum* 62, no. 2 (February 1935), pp. 20 and 40 (supplement)./Esso rotary station, New York. *National Petroleum News*

(February 5, 1936), p. 328./Martin Greif, *Depression Modern: The Thirties Style in America* (New York: Universe Books, 1975), p. 84.

(p. 69)   Texaco prototype model designed by Walter Dorwin Teague

"Planning Techniques for New and Remodeled Buildings," *The Architectural Forum* 66, no. 2 (February 1937), p. 92./"Standardized Service Stations Designed by Walter Dorwin Teague," *The Architectural Record* 82, no. 3 (September 1937), p. 69–72.

(p. 72)   a gas station in Palo Alto, California

"Modern Service Station, Stanford University Campus," *The Architect and Engineer* 214, no. 1 (July 1958), p. 7.

(p. 72)   Eliot Noyes created a widely implemented design

"Stores: Building Types Study #370: Architecture for Selling—Prototype for Service Stations: Mobil Tests Effect of Design on Sale at 58 Locations," *The Architectural Record* 141, no. 5 (May 1967), pp. 172–173./ " 'O' Come Ruota," *Domes* 506 (January 1972), p. 41./"Mobil," *Architecture Plus* 1, no. 6 (July 1973), pp. 50–54.

(p. 75)   Vincent G. Kling & Associates designed . . . a prototype

"Updating the Service Station Image," *Industrial Design* 12, no. 8 (August 1965), p. 45.

(p. 75)   Miës van der Rohe . . . addressed the problem of the drive-in building

Peter Carter, *Miës van der Rohe At Work* (New York: Praeger Publishers, 1974), pp. 185–193.

(p. 75)   station-restaurant combination along the Tri-State Toll Road in Illinois

"Highway Restaurant and Service Station, David Haid, Architect," *Arts and Architecture* 83 (January 1967), pp. 16–17./Highway Service Station, Illinois," *Architectural Design* 38, no. 4 (April 1968), pp. 185–186./"Rest Stop—1,000 Feet Ahead in Quality," *The Architectural Forum* 129, no. 2 (September 1968), pp. 75–79.

(p. 75)   an award-winning station of 1973 designed by Lawrence Booth

"Prototype Gas Station Looks Like A Winner—And Is," *Progressive Architecture* 53, no. 10 (October 1972), p. 31./Stuart E. Cohen, "A Chicago School Filling Station, not Pumping Pop," *Inland Architect* (July 1973), pp. 16–19./Stuart E. Cohen, *Chicago Architects* (Chicago: Swallow Press, 1976), pp. 24 and 89.

(p. 79)   American preservation in its early years

A comprehensive history of the American preservation movement can be found in: Charles B. Homer, Jr., *Presence of the Past: A History of the Preservation Movement in the United States Before Williamsburg* (New York: G. P. Putnam's Sons, 1965)./At the National Trust for Historic Preservation 1973 annual meeting in Boston, a session was held on roadside architecture. Chaired by Peter H. Smith, the session included presentations by designer Richard J. S. Gutman of Cambridge, Massachusetts, and by Paul W. Ivory, administrator of Chesterwood, a National Trust property in Stockbridge, Massachusetts./Joanne Ditmer, "Raising the Roof: Automotive Artifacts Vanishing." *Denver Post* (October 29, 1975)./Phil Langdon, "Before They Vanish—Saving Gas Stations, Diners and Other Examples of Mass-produced Architecture 30 and 40 Years Ago is the Object of New Preservationists," *Buffalo Evening News/Gusto* (July 21, 1978), pp. 10–11.

(p. 80)   HABS-HAER

Historical Sites Act of 1935 (Public Law 292). Harley J. McKee, *Recording Historic Buildings* (US Department of the Interior–National Parks Service, 1970), p. 1.

(p. 82)   Wadham's Oil Company station as a local trademark

Mark A. Latus, *Wisconsin Inventory of Historic Places*, 1973./Mark A. Latus and Mary Ellen Young, *Milwaukee County Directory of Historic Places*, 1973 (See Chapter 2, Fig. 31.)

(p. 82)   shell-shaped station

Brent Glass and Mary Alice Hinson, National Register of Historic Places nominating form (October 30, 1975). (See Chapter 2, Fig. 24.)

(p. 82)   Lemmon, South Dakota's Petrified Park

Scott Gerloff, National Register of Historic Places nominating form (December 1975). (See Chapter 2, page 20.)

(p. 82)   E. W. Norris service station

Richard Pankratz and Cornelia Wyman, National Register of Historic Places nominating form (August 1976). (See Chapter 2, Fig. 27.)

104

(p. 82) One of these Respectable stations located in Greenwich Village, New York

MARY B. DIERICK, National Register of Historic Places nominating form (1975).

(p. 82) "Functional" brick box, Fayetteville, Arkansas

CURTIS PRESLEY, National Register of Historic Places nominating form (May 1977).

(p. 82) Examples of preservation and rehabilitation

JAMES MARSTON FITCH, "Conceptual Parameters of Preservation" (unpublished paper).

(p. 82) Respectable neoclassical Gulf Station in Washington, DC

J. Y. SMITH, "NW Gas Station Will Be Preserved," *The Washington Post* (April 27, 1973). (See Chapter 3.)

(p. 82) the Fantastic teapot station . . . has been moved

"Teapot To Be Fixed, Moved," *Tri-City Herald,* Pasco, Washington (August 17, 1977). (See Chapter 2.)

(p. 83) Tarrytown, New York, inn became the Headless Horseman station

"Station Revives Ichabod Crane's Love Affair," *National Petroleum News* (August 28, 1929), p. 88. (See Chapter 2.)

(p. 85) Albert L. Kerth . . . recently wrote a book

ALBERT L. KERTH, *A New Life for the Abandoned Service Station* (Massapequa Park, N.Y.: A. L. KERTH, 1974).

(p. 85) adaptive reuse of abandoned stations

ANDREW KAPOCIUNAS, "Old Gas Stations Are Something Else—How to find new uses for abandoned service stations and save a bundle!" *Capitalist Reporter* (December 1973), pp. 48–50./D'ARCY O'CONNOR, "Entrepreneurs Find Ex-Gasoline Stations Can Have New Uses," *The Wall Street Journal,* (no date). Reprinted by the New York State Council on Architecture (July 1974)./Mimi Crossley, "New Stations In Life," *The Houston Post* (October 22, 1978), pp. 1 and 20BB./ROBERT FRAUSTO, "Gas Stations Pull a Quick-Change Act," *Planning* (American Society of Planning Officials, December 1974).

Sources and Notes for Illustrations

1 Beginnings

FIG. 1. 1890s Sun Oil bulk plant, Detroit, Michigan. Courtesy Sun Oil Company.

FIG. 2: Refueling in 1901. Courtesy Bain Collection, Library of Congress.

FIG. 3: C. H. Laessig (extreme left) and crew at his Automobile Gasoline Company, St. Louis, Missouri, 1905. *National Petroleum News* (February 5, 1936), p. 205.

FIGS. 4 & 5: Advertisement of Correct Measure Company, Rochester, Pennsylvania. *National Petroleum News* 21, no. 51 (December 18, 1929). Author's collection.

FIG. 6: 1920s Texaco station, Hartford Garage Company, Hartford, Connecticut. Courtesy Texaco, Inc.

FIG. 7: 1910 retail gas station, Automobile Gasoline Company, St. Louis, Missouri.

FIG. 8: Split-pump station. Courtesy Sun Oil Company.

FIG. 9: Uniformed Texaco station attendant. Courtesy *National Petroleum News*.

FIG. 10: Uniformed Conoco station attendant. Courtesy Continental Oil Company.

FIG. 11: Lubritorium. Courtesy Sun Oil Company.

FIG. 12: 1910 Central Oil Company station and bulk plant, Detroit, Michigan. Courtesy *National Petroleum News*.

FIG. 13: Gulf self-service prototype, Houston, Texas, 1978. Stephen Edward Moskowitz, photographer. Author's collection.

FIG. 14: Dry goods store–filling station, Onondaga, New York. Courtesy Shell Oil Company.

FIG. 15: U-Tote-M store and filling station, Houston, Texas, 1978. Photo by author. Author's collection.

FIG. 16: Maps offered at a 1934 Gulf station. Courtesy New York Public Library.

FIG. 17: 1930 Gulf Refining Company credit card. Courtesy Gulf Oil Corporation.

2 The Fantastic

FIG. 18: Airplane station. Courtesy Gulf Oil Corporation.

FIG. 19: 1933 Lighthouse station, Huntington, New York. Courtesy Mobil Oil Corporation.

FIG. 20: 1940s Lighthouse station, Miami Beach, Florida. Courtesy Gulf Oil Corporation.

FIG. 21: 1960s Sinclair Dino gas pump. Courtesy *National Petroleum News*.

FIG. 22: "Space" station, Atlanta, Georgia, 1979. Meda Moultrie Dubose, photographer. Author's collection.

FIG. 23: Gallon Measure service station, Buchanan, New York, 1976. Photo by author. Author's collection.

FIG. 24: 1930s shell-shaped station, Winston-Salem, North Carolina, 1975. Courtesy Jo Ann Sieburg, photographer.

FIG. 25: "Tree" station, San Antonio, Texas, 1978. Photo by author. Author's collection.

FIG. 26: "Mammy" station, US Highway 61, near Natchez, Mississippi. Courtesy Thomas Jefferson Eby III, photographer.

3 The Respectable

4 The Domestic